# DREAM CARS

SERGE BELLU . PETER VANN

# DREAM CARS
## Style for Tomorrow

*Motorbooks International*
Publishers & Wholesalers Inc
®

# ACKNOWLEDGEMENTS

Thin book already has a long history. Its origins go back to the time when Peter and I were doing our first reporting. Throughout those years, we roamed the length and breadth of Europe to find the best examples of our "dream car". As the years rolled by, I also came to know Peter. Today, I know that for him, this book is a homage to an absent person who was torn away from him. In times gone by, Ursula was at his side, revealing his art to him and offering encouragement.

We have relied on trusty accomplices to construct the framework of our reverie. On the ground, Christian Garnier-Collot allowed Peter to make use of his passion for design and helped him with all the photographs.

Claudine Renaux's keen eye picked out the most striking images and put them together with elegance and discretion. Martin Santoni helped me with the writing, supervising the documentation and editing with pertinent and wise insight.

At E.P.A., Anne-Marie Veujoz and Antoine Prunet watched over the final drafting of the text with their customary tact and attention to detail, while Gilles Blanchet orchestrated the production of the book.

We would like to thank all the designers and stylists and all the staff of the research departments who helped us. Most of the people mentioned in the book welcomed us with patience, understanding and often with enthusiasm. Our gratitude also goes out to the communications men and women who acted as interpreters for us with the creators: Uwe Brotbeck, Daniela Cappa, Humbert Emmanuel Carcel, Gérard Chainet, Christian Chauvin, Luca Ciferi, Thomas Einkammerer, Patrick Garnier, Yves Guittet, Ottmar Kup, Michèle Marchiano, Gianbeppe Panicco, France Pagnot, Lorenza Pininfarina, Ruzena Sanak, Jean-Pierre Thibault, Marie-Thérèse Trouvé, Renato Ughi, Fredi Valentini and Serge Van Hove. Our gratitude also goes out to the National Automobile Museum in Mulhouse and the Kodak company.

Finally, we would like to acknowledge the cordial cooperation of Gianni Bulgari, Fulvio Cinti, Joseph Henry, Alberto Martinez, Hector Obalk and Shizuo Takashima.

As this book is intended to open a window on to the future, we are dedicating it to Charlotte, Oscar, Justine and Lisa, who all came into the world during the 1980s.

*This edition published in 1989 by Motorbooks International Publishers & Wholesalers, Inc., PO Box 2, Osceola, WI 54020 USA*

*First published by Éditions E.P.A. Paris 1989 as Le Rêve Automobile: Le style des annees 80*

*© Éditions E.P.A Paris 1988*

*Printed and bound in Spain by Cayfosa, Barcelona*

*The information in this book is true and complete to the best of our knowledge. All recommendations are made without any guarantee on the part of the author or publisher, who also disclaim any liability incurred in connection with the use of this data or specific details.*

*We recognize that some words, model names and designations, for example, mentioned herein are the property of the trademark holder. We use them for identification purposes only. This is not an official publication.*

*Library of Congress Cataloguing-in-Publication Data*

*Vann, Peter.*
  *[Rêve automobile.      English]*
  *Dream cars / Peter Vann, Serge Bellu.*
      *p.        cm.*
    *ISBN 0-87938-364-X*
    *1. Automobiles——Miscellanea.      I. Bellu, Serge.      II. Title.*
*TL154.V3513      1989*
*629.222——dc20*
                                                              *89-8235*
                                                                  *CIP*

# SUMMARY

"If you want fresh ideas, you have to change them every day, just as you change your shirt", as Francis Picabia used to say. This dada-iste precept could be used as a caption for the twists and turns of the 1980s.

By their very nature, cars are full of contradictions. Designers are hamstrung by legal, commercial, technological and financial constraints. Cars, more than any other industrial object, are governed by subjective impulses at every stage: from the moment of conception right up to when the motorist chooses one and buys it. Cars are truly objects of sensibility and imagination. People who create them must combine emotions and symbols. They also have to work with the public capacity to assimilate innovation. Cars vary according to geography and culture. Stylists and designers express their most committed ideas in "dream cars", superb butterflies which live no longer than a Car Show. We have decided to use these rare and ephemeral automobiles to illustrate this book on the style of the 1980s. These cars are at the forefront of creativity, they are the foretaste of things to come, they are not forced to fit the bland mould dictated by marketing; they are, in their way, a eulogy of perfection.

But why "the 1980s"? Why impose this cut-off? Simply because the 20th century has been broken into decades by world events. The Twenties were heady with rediscovered peace, the Thirties were bracketed between depression and war. The 1980s blossomed as they moved away from the 1979 crisis which erupted six years after the first oil price shock. Economic conditions have set off changes in society which designers have had to reflect. This ferment has produced five trends which have marked contemporary design.

## Aerodynamics: from crisis to optimism

Aerodynamics is the buzzword of our era, but our understanding of it has evolved throughout the decade. Initially the motivations for aerodynamics were economic. Concern for energy conservation took its place alongside safety and anti-pollution, and manufacturers took them to heart. With the approval of "Energy Saving Agencies", France and Germany witnessed the arrival of prototypes designed with the sole objective of reducing consumption. This psychosis had positive effects on research into aerodynamics and weight reduction, on the discovery of new materials and on production methods. However, cars cannot be separated for any length of time from their play and fantasy functions. The reaction came around 1984 from the United States and Japan, where dream cars once again assumed an allure that was more fantastic than pragmatic. They were draped in lines inspired by Nature and their designers took account of the precepts of bio-design laid down by Luigi Colani. The laws of aerodynamics took a new turn towards other, more optimistic destinations.

## Postmodernism or glimpses of timelessness

In architecture, postmodernism was a way of reacting against austerity and uniformity. This baroque and whimsical aesthetic, with its liberal sprinkling of historical references, put an end to the often totalitarian rigour advocated by the sons of Bauhaus. Under the banner of Postmodernism, architecture once again flirted with the vernacular charms which had been erased by the International Style. The process was similar in cars. The frantic pursuit of aerodynamics could have ended up as uniformity. People wondered whether all cars had come from the same mould made by the C.A.O. But the act of creation is always stimulated by emotional and cultural influences. Many creators continue to defend a school of body design which is firmly outside the bounds of functionalism.

Sometimes the postmodernist game turns into caricature, the vocabulary is peppered with history and humour. Some models are adorned with emblems from the Fifties and Sixties in a spirit which is more subversive than nostalgic, thereby rejecting the symbols of a society attached to luxury and gloss. We have witnessed the resurgence of the Fifties in American culture. Aluminium diners are back in business again. Amidst the under-age *preppies* and an indifferent *middle class*, a few *funkies* spread their romanticism along the naugahide wall sofas and feel

**"Using functionalism to solve the problems of existence is an outmoded idea; these days design is becoming more sensual, meaning that the things which are designed and produced tend more to be perceived by the senses than by the intellect." Ettore Sottsass, 1985.**

amused at how *period* they are. Didn't somebody once say that the style of the Eighties was the style of the Fifties added to the style of the Thirties?

## The advocates of Individualism

Individualism is a trend which has become more insistent since the beginning of the decade in reaction to the crisis. It is marked by a refusal to become absorbed into the mass of society, and "special series" cars have developed alongside mass production models in the same way that the proliferation of hypermarkets has seen the parallel rise of individual boutiques. "Microcultural" diversification has changed the nature of consumption and industry must be prepared to respond to a broader range of demands. Several sports car projects are prepared to pander to a brand of individualism which borders on egomania; these are car-toys with the emphasis on arousing passion by stirring up childhood emotions. This "quality of life" approach is typical of our era, so it is not surprising that many firms are emphasising the sensual over the pragmatic in the form of sports cars. With shades of the memory of the *spider* of James Dean — a silver speck which disappeared one evening at the edge of the desert, somewhere down Salinas way. Taking off into the wind and freedom.

But this approach has to take ecology into account. So to make people feel less guilty, the idea of bringing Man and Nature together has given birth to cross-country vehicles and the prospect of a new race of all-purpose machines with mixed roots in sports, town, working and adventure vehicles. These mutants are a cross between World War II Jeeps and the Paris-Dakar *bolides*. Another example of the ability of cars to invent new disguises.

"Fashion is created by followers. Unlike art, it is a creation of the masses". Hector Obalk, 1984.

"Some of the most aberrant deviations in cars have been perpetrated in the name of 'styling'. It took the trauma of the oil crisis to make the word 'styling', with its connotations of marketing and opportunism, finally disappear from research departments; only then did the distinction between 'styling' and 'design' become clear. In contrast, design works with technology, economics, ergonomics and even symbolism. Aerodynamics left a deep mark on the design of the 80s: for some people, it was an excuse used to justify several 'atrocities', while others who were able to master the science used it as a creative tool. In these instances, cars can claim to be moving sculptures." Fulvio Cinti, 1988.

## Functionalism freed from the sharpness of high tech.

"Functional" cars came out of the closet during the Sixties. Twenty years later, designers were able to create special, large-capacity cars – "minivans" in the USA. Once again, social trends were behind the birth of a new species of car. At a time when a new idea of "families" has emerged, these cars with plenty of room for conviviality have naturally found their niche. Even so, this type of car is still of marginal appeal because its functional character is too close to the high-tech spirit. Shifts in fashion have lead to Bio-design and Postmodernism taking the edge off the sharpest forms of design. We are gradually moving towards a traveller's vehicle in which the ideas of comfort, conviviality and space reign supreme but which seduces with graceful lines breaking any link with a utilitarian past.

## Neoclassical aspirations

The lurches of history often provoke a return to conservative values. Conservatives defend their territory against the encroachment of progressive currents. Since the mid-Seventies, this trend has managed to dam up the modernist leanings of the post-war era. Returning to "traditional values" is one of the most reassuring ways of escaping from the crisis, and cars have not escaped the return to tradition. For many people they are still a status symbol. Winds of change might have brought in new ideas in the form of multi-purpose styling, but the appeal of the so-called "classic" limousine style is still indissolubly bound up with the idea of luxury and respectability.

If you read through the annals of industrial creations, you will find numerous examples of these tendencies. As Picabia once wrote, "masterpieces are nothing more than documents."

Maybe some of these cars are nothing more than masterpieces.

"Cars came about as a means of transport and for many years were designed and bought as such. Since all cars are required to provide us with a certain level of service, and since the number of cars is greater than the number of buyers, the challenge to manufacturers looks more and more like a game of seduction. Cars, like fashion, tend to forget their primary purpose and instead go for pleasure, emotion, intangible attributes: they are moving out of 'high-tech' into 'high-touch'. Whereas technological advances tend to homogenise products, the outward appearance and image has to be the distinguishing mark which ultimately motivates people to buy. It's no longer the function which creates the form, but rather the form itself which becomes the actual function.' Gianni Bulgari, 1988.

"There are no neutral feelings between the driver and engineering. Desire and pleasure always try to go beyond utility." Hervé Poulain, 1986.

Italian bodywork had its head in the clouds for many years, with no competitors and no challenges. These days, it has to accept comparison – with the Japanese, who are proud to have broken loose – with the Americans, who are feeling heady with the turnaround of their car industry. Do Italian bodywork stylists have what it takes to emerge unscathed?

Nuccio Bertone is carrying on the tradition of Italian bodywork styling with designs such as Ramarro. This is a working prototype built on the basis of a Chevrolet Corvette. It keeps the same wheelbase but the length is reduced from 4.48 to 4.15 metres. The Ramarro was presented in May 1984 as part of the Los Angeles Auto Expo.

**With his serious mask of a face heavy with half a century of contributions to history, Nuccio Bertone is constantly peering into the future.**

Citroën BX Paris September 1982. With its angular lines, it is still firmly rooted in the Seventies. This preliminary design dates from 1979.

Mazda MX-81 Tokyo. October 1981. Prototype based on Mazda 323 Turbo ordered by Togyo Kogyo. Inside, the steering wheel is replaced by a belt running round a television screen that provides the driver with essential information.

Less than an hour separates two opposite but complementary worlds. One is the Turin suburb of Grugliasco, with its dreary, dirty streets laid out on a grid pattern; this is the location of the Bertone factory, set amid ageing Sixties architecture. The other, one hundred kilometres away in the Susa valley at the foothills of the Alps is Caprie, setting for a light and peaceful research centre. These are the two poles of Bertone's life: bodywork and styling. "Three times a week I head off to Caprie, I leave the cares of industry behind and return to the calm and optimism of creating".

It was in the immediate post-war period when Nuccio Bertone took (born 1914) took over the running of the firm which his father had founded in 1912. As the Seventies dawned, Bertone decided to separate the research centre and the production plant. As he saw it, designers working in the factory were pestered too much by the unions and all the obstacles they raised. These days Bertone has a somewhat bitter memory of the years following 1968, when workers besieged his office . . . By moving the research centre in 1974 and giving it its administrative and geographical independence, Bertone intended to shelter the creative work from socio-political storms. The department started off as Stile SA and later became Stile Bertone in early 1985. It is run by a general manager and comprises two branches: exterior styling and interior styling. Peace has returned to Grugliasco but Bertone was profoundly shaken by the second oil shock. Having thrown in his lot with Italian manufacturers, he suddenly found himself out on a limb when they reacted to the economic crisis by increasingly making do without their sub-contractors. Like his colleagues and indeed, like the whole Turin area, Bertone was too deeply dependent on almighty Fiat. He forged new alliances, which resulted in design and production of the Volvo 780 and the Opel Kadett. These links are an industrial shield for Bertone, who provides a livelihood for the 1,500 workers employed in the Grugliasco and Caselle factories. Huge investments have been made in this sector: electrophoresis has been introduced in the paint shop and a building of 15,000 square metres has been constructed to

add to the existing 70,000 square metres under cover.

But the bodywork stylist's "raison d'être", indeed his passion in life, is pure creation. This is a field in which Bertone has strengthened his cooperative work with several major manufacturers, pursuing a policy of forging relations with only one firm per country. In France, his work with Citroën gave rise to the BX and its successor the CX. In Japan, Mazda is Bertone's faithful partner. New countries are waking up to the possibilities of styling, and this could be a breath of fresh air for independent creators living in a saturated European market. Eastern-bloc and Far Eastern countries are now demanding "style" so that they can get a foothold in the West. This is why Skoda consulted Bertone for the design of the Favorit saloon car.

Taking a long, hard look at Bertone, it is tempting to think that he has missed out on several major historical trends by following a different path from his colleagues. Just look at the Show prototypes presented during the Eighties. With Bertone there was no record *Cx* aerodynamic saloon, no high-profile utility vehicle. The theme running through the Athon (1980), the Delfino (1983), the Ramarro (1984), the Zabrus (1985) and the Genesis (1988) is a dream; none of these projects had anything industrial about them and they were all based on high-performance engineering – the Lamborghini V8, Alfa 6, Corvette, Citroen BX 4TC and Lamborghini V12.

Bertone goes very much against the ideologues of design by putting all the emphasis on style, on pure aesthetics. The interplay of proportions, light, surface contours and the finishing of details, the link between planes is as important as the overall concept, if not more so. Nuccio Bertone is neither a stylist nor a designer, but rather a *coachbuilder* in the original sense of the word. However, to look at the details of his creations is to discover many original solutions in the layout of the driver's position, the way the doors open, the integration of the windows into the bodywork. In the Zabrus and the Genesis, Bertone explored new ways forward for Gran Turismo cars. With its functional rear end, the Zabrus is as much of an estate as it is a coupé. As for the hatchback Genesis, it aims to move the brute

Above: <u>Delfino</u>, Geneva, 1983. Four-seater coupé based on the mechanics of Alfa 6, V6 engine, 2.5 litres. 165 hp, length 414 cm.

Below: <u>Athon</u>, Geneva, 1981. Spider based on Lamborghini Urraco mechanics, V8 3-litre engine, 280 hp, length 397 cm.

Below and following double page: <u>Ramarro</u>, Los Angeles, May 1984. It uses a type of leather suggested by its name – green lizard skin.

selfishness of a Turismo saloon towards something more comfortable and cosy

## The art of Coachbuilding

The Caprie workshops are able to produce whole prototypes, everything from metalwork to glasswork, from upholstery to paintwork. There are just fifteen or so stylists among the 80 people who work here. Bertone recruits them locally and before they become stylists, candidates have to do all the other jobs. "We prefer to train our own young people and steep them in car culture on the spot; technical knowledge is essential for a stylist," Nuccio Bertone insists.

The man who has been responsible for style since 1979 is a small, shy Frenchman, Marc Deschamps, who hides behind a beard and glasses. Born in 1944, he came into this job by chance. After graduating from high school, he started off at Peugeot, put in a spell at Ligier, then went into Régie Renault in 1975. At Bertone, Marc Deschamps is the latest in a series of extraordinary men: Franco Scaglione (1952-1960) with his exuberant talent, Giorgetto Giugiaro (1960-1965) and Marcello Gandini (1965-1979).

One of Nuccio Bertone's undoubted strengths is his instinct for sniffing out talent and bringing it to fruit. He has the leader's great talent for surrounding himself with exceptional helpers. It is through these strong and dissimilar personalities that Nuccio ensures the continuity of that style which is so distinctively . . . Bertone.

<u>Zabrus,</u> Turin 1986. Design for a functional sports coupé based on the Citroën BX 4TC; 2.1 litre 200 hp turbo engine, four-wheel drive, length 430 cm.

On the Zabrus, the cut of
the glass surfaces and the
complex contouring of the
side body panels shows
that the mastery of the
stylists is perfectly
translated by the mastery of
the coachbuilders.

Following double page:
Genesis, Turin 1988. A new
look for the touring car – a
high (152 cm) and short (447
cm) hatchback body with
room for five people;
engine Lamborghini V12.

**The term "coachbuilder" is too restrictive for Pininfarina. Admittedly, it has all the connotations of a noble craft, but on the other hand it does not do justice to the technological dimension.**

Pininfarina's art can be seen equally well in the classic lines of the Ferrari Pinin saloon (1980) which was intended for production, and in the aerodynamic perfection of the PF-CNR model (1978).

W hen Pininfarina opened his new study and research centre in Cambiano on 24 April 1982, Pininfarina was making a clear statement: it was time for Italian coachwork to move into top gear. The time of craftsmen was past, the metal-worker tapping aluminium to shape a wing was a distant memory. Pininfarina had long since distinguished himself from his colleagues by pursuing technical progress. The first Centro Studi e Ricerche inaugurated in March 1966 at Grugliasco was the crowning glory of Battista Pininfarina's work. Just one month later, this great figure in Italian coachbuilding passed away in Lausanne at the age of seventy-three. After following his brother Giovanni into Stabilimenti Farina, Battista Farina struck out on his own in 1930 to found Carrozzeria Pinin Farina (it was not until 1961 that his diminutive name, Pinin, was officially tagged on to his family name – by presidential decree). Battista Pininfarina made a decisive contribution to the development of Italian coachbuilding. Whenever history came to a crossroads, he somehow managed to point his firm in the right direction. In the early Twenties, this self-taught man from Piedmont went to the United States on a trip to familiarise himself with modern production methods. After the war, he established new, closer relationships between coachbuilders and car manufacturers, providing for collaboration from the drawing board to the production line. The famous Cisitalia 202, which is on display at the Museum of Modern Art in New York, was born of this interaction. Pininfarina went on to build on these new bases, establishing durable links with a number of firms including Lancia, Alfa Romeo, Peugeot, BMC and of course, Ferrari.

On the death of Battista Pininfarina, his son Sergio took over just as he was turning forty. With his engineering training, he was able to complement his father's work by developing the technological side of the firm. The wind tunnel designed by Alberto Morelli was completed in November 1972; one of the

Brio, Geneva, 1983. Coup which Pininfarina wanted to market under his own name; Fiat Ritmo Abarth 125 TC engine, 4 cylinders, 1,995 cc, 125 hp, Cx 0.29.

first projects to emerge from this wind tunnel was the Ferrari Studio CR 25 with a Cx of 0.256 – remarkable for 1974. The aerodynamic reference point was to become the CNR-PF revealed at the Turin motor show in 1978. Financed by the National Research Council, this ideal form was destined to leave a deep impression amidst the alarm of the energy crisis. The model scored a Cx of 0.172 with all the usefulness of an average family saloon.

With Pininfarina, as with most of his fellow designers, each prototype unveiled at motor shows is in homage to work with a given manufacturer. For instance, the Studio-HPX was in honour of the cooperation between Honda and the coachbuilders for the City convertible project. A year later, the elegant Griffe 4 celebrated twenty years of cooperation with Peugeot. Ever since the 403, all the cars coming out of Sochaux have in fact been the result of constructive competition between the French stylists and Pininfarina. In some cases, such as the 205 and the 405, their complicity was so extensive that the final product ended up being a mixture of all their proposals. In parallel with this, Industrie Pininfarina SpA built the 404, 504, Samba and 205 convertibles and the 404 and 504 coupés on the Grugliasco production lines.

On the industrial front, we cannot fail to mention the unprecedented operation undertaken with General Motors. Cadillac needed a top-quality name on its Allant convertible if it was to compete with Mercedes-Benz and Jaguar. Pininfarina had long been associated with GM and was chosen to design a prestige model; it set up an impressive plant to produce it. A new factory was built in San Giorgio Canavese near Turin and an air lift was arranged three times per week between the Piedmontese capital and Detroit, where the mechanical part of the car was installed. Unfortunately, the paths to success in America are impenetrable; the commercial success of the car fell far short of the costs incurred and the Cadillac Allanté was given the unen-

Quartz, Geneva 1981. Coup dedicated to the Swiss *Revue Automobile* on the occasion of its 75th anniversary. Chassis Audi Quattro, 5 cylinders, 2.2 litres turbo, 200 hp, elliptical optic lights designed by Carello.

viable accolade of "flop of the year" in 1987 before it disappeared. Fortunately, in the same year Pininfarina was awarded the "Car Design Award" for the design of the Alfa 164 (this prize brings together 10 representatives of the international press and has been organised since 1983 at the initiative of Turin city council, the region of Piedmont and the magazine *Auto & Design*).

Opposite and previous double page: <u>Studio HPX,</u> Turin 1984. Project based on a Honda RA264E formula 2 engine, V8 1996 cc. Aerodynamic bodywork using ground effect.

Above: Ferrari 288 GTO,
Geneva 1984. Engine V8
turbo 2.8 litres 400 hp.
Previous double page and
below: Ferrari Testarossa,

Paris 1984. Bodywork made
of aluminium except for
steel doors, 12 cylinder
engine, 5 litres, 390 hp.

The most accomplished fusion of a motor manufacturer and a coachbuilder has been achieved in the association of Ferrari and Pininfarina. The Ferrari legend would never have been sublimated into myth without the art of Pininfarina. Without the coachbuilder, the Ferrari legend would have been nothing more than an unfinished story. This marriage of art, speed and technology has been going since 1952 and continues to produce monuments. The Testarossa, which was presented at the 1984 Paris Motor Show, will without a doubt go down in the golden annals of Ferrari-Pininfarina collaboration. The coachbuilder set himself the task of integrating the aerodynamics into the overall body sculpture without leaving any slight projections; the stylists managed to achieve this by paying the utmost attention to detail on the mirrors, the front air intake and the area of turbulence above the engine. This theme was pursued with a "NACA" air intake and the rear spoiler.

The creation of a new sports category in 1982 gave rise to a new breed of very particular cars which prompted unprecedented commercial practices. In fact, 200 models had to be produced to qualify for "Group B" and race in world championship rallies. This random figure was a nuisance for big factories, which found themselves committed to producing a limited series offering little profit. However, other firms found they had struck gold in the form of exclusive, élite cars. Porsche and Ferrari announced the creation of the 959 and the 288 GTO as potential racing cars intended to be ratified for Group B. In reality, these exceptional cars with their unlikely sporting prospects have become the most desirable touring cars of the age. To create the 288 GTO, all Pininfarina had to do was expand on the form of the 308 GTB. Scaglietti produced 272 models instead of the 200 initially promised. In view of the success of these cars and the capital growth immediately enjoyed by their owners, Ferrari and Pininfarina decided to recreate a similar event and developed the F40 which was unveiled during the summer of 1987. Pininfarina used a completely

Cadillac Allanté, Paris 1986.
Joint venture between
Pininfarina and General
Motors. V8 engine, 4.1
litres, 170 hp.

different signature, even though they started from the basis of the GTO. This time the task was no longer to erase the aerodynamic accessories, but rather to accentuate them, thereby translating the refinement of the car's technology into aggressive styling. Unfortunately these thoroughbreds were spoiled by the speculation which surrounded them and by uncertainty about what they were meant to be. However, the legacy that remains beyond all this ambiguity is the result of some magnificent technical research. The structure of the F40 comprises a tubular chassis reinforced with composite materials.

This line of research was confirmed by the Hit, a coupé unveiled at the 1988 Turin Motor Show and built on the mechanical basis of the Lancia Delta HF Integrale. It was mounted on a carbon fibre composite platform, sober and deep, which is in turn used as a decorative element in the dashboard. From the aesthetic point of view, the Hit refrained from being dashing and from boasting its aerodynamic qualities; it was in the tradition of the 1981 Audi Quartz and the 1982 Fiat Brio. With Pininfarina, style is often eclipsed by technology; innovation is covered so discreetly that in time, it becomes classical.

This tendency was no doubt encouraged by Leonardo Fioravanti, who held the reins at the Centro Studi e Ricerche from 1972. A graduate of the Milan Polytechnical School, Fioravanti has always approached style with the feelings of an engineer. In January 1988, at the time of his fiftieth birthday, he left Pininfarina to go back to Ferrari's research department. His righthand man Lorenzo Ramaciotti took over as the new boss at Cambiano.

This opened a new chapter in the story of Pininfarina, which was financially consecrated in August 1986 in a stock market flotation. On every front Sergio Pininfarina, the "top boss" of Italian bosses, has transformed the company created by his father; he makes use of the resources available to modern industry without disregarding the fruits of tradition.

Ferrari F40, July 1987.
Limited series small saloon,
V8 turbo engine, 3 litres, 478
hp, 324 kph.

Griffe 4, Geneva 1985.
Design for Peugeot 205
coupé to commemorate 30
years of cooperation with
the French manufacturer.

Vivace, Turin 1988. Alfa
Romeo ordered two mockups, one a coupé and the
other a sports version, both
based on the mechanics of
the 164. Moreover the front
part was a foretaste of the
saloon.
Following double page: Hit,
Turin 1988.

<u>Hit,</u> Turin 1988. Prototype based on the Lancia Delta HF Integrale – study of intensive use of composite materials (Sandwich of Nomex honeycomb panels and carbon fibre sheets).

Weight of the platform: 40 kg, Cx 0.29

**Giorgetto Giugiaro is even more famous than his own brand, Ital Design, and has emerged as the key figure in car design over the last twenty years. His detractors refer to him as often as his supporters.**

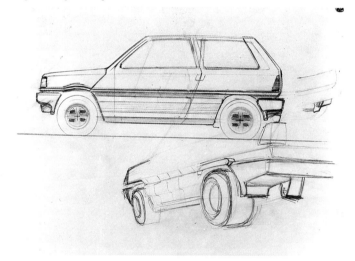

Sketches for the Fiat Panda, signed Giorgetto Giugiaro.

The interior of the Lancia Delta as seen by Syd Mead, the American science fiction illustrator, author of the book *Sentinel* and design consultant to the film *Blade Runner*.

I t takes an artistic temperament to understand the development of cars outside a technological context." With this remark, Giorgetto Giugiaro is blowing his own trumpet – he studied at the Turin Academy of Fine Art – and also contradicting the "integrational" line of thought, which has a clear tendency to reject the artistic roots of design and to glorify its scientific foundation. Giugiaro became familiar with plastic arts at a very early age. In Garessio, Giugiaro's father Mario used to paint landscapes. In fact, it was he who painted the fresco on the ceiling of a small village church about one hundred kilometres from Turin. Throughout his adolescence, art was part of Giugiaro's daily fare amid the Piedmontese hills where he was born on 7 August 1938.

"I also did a technical design course and it was this experience which gave me a second chance of success in industry", is how Giugiaro excuses his natural artistic leanings. He prefers to recruit young people who have technical training and artistic sensibility rather than artists who have to be taught the disciplines of a technician. When Giugiaro formed his company in February 1968, he made sure that he could call on the help of a group of technicians: Gino Boaretti, Luciano Bosio and Aldo Mantovani. Only the last one, Giugiaro's trusty friend, is still part of the management structure of SIRP SpA (Studi Industriali Realisazzione Prototipi SpA), the registered name of Ital Design. It is Mantovani who operates from the wings to provide the technical counterweight in Ital Design's management duo.

What immediately distinguishes this company from traditional coachbuilders is that they offer manufacturers complete projects in which both the mechanical and the stylistic aspects are carefully worked out. This approach is illustrated by

Previous page and above:
Medusa, Turin 1980.
Aerodynamic saloon built
on the chassis of an
elongated Lancia Monte
Carlo; 4 cylinder engine,
1995 cc, 120 hp, wheelbase
279 cm, length 440 cm. Cx
0.23.

the Maya. It was designed for Ford in 1984 and developed with
a view to producing it in small numbers and marketing it in
North America. A first mock-up was shown at the 1984 Turin
Motor Show, then the following year, a more developed version,
the Maya IIES was built and followed by a working prototype
(Maya IIEM) fitted with a central engine mounted lengthwise
(and not transversely as on the first prototypes). This project
(under the designation GN34) was salvaged for a few months
by the French company Chausson, but was finally dropped by
Ford in 1986.

Unlike its competitors, Ital Design has always refused to make the move into mass production (an exception was made for the BMW M1). Still, Ital Design can handle the manufacture of several dozen prototypes, as it did for the Merkur XR4TI, the American version of the Ford Sierra.

Giorgetto Giugiaro is always more of an artist than an industrialist; he is intimately involved with the creative processes and his personalised style has made a major contribution to the fame of Ital Design. The whole world comes to consult him. For many people he is a key reference point, a guarantee of being in touch with international trends. Saab, Lancia and Fiat gave him the job of designing their related saloon cars, the 9000, Thema and Croma, so that they could be sure of having different characters despite having exactly the same basic structure on the three cars. The Gabbiano prototype (1983) with its gull wings marked the start of the collaboration between Giugiaro and Régie Renault who asked him to finish off the 21, create the Eagle Premier, design the 19 and in each case, to satisfy a conservative market. Commercially, going for the banal often pays off; it is popular with marketing men who hold "clinics",

Preceding double page:
<u>Capsula,</u> Turin 1982. All-round vehicle based on Alfasud mechanical design, length 372 cm, height 166 cm.
Below: <u>Orca,</u> Turin 1982. Saloon on Lancia Delta Turbo 4x4 base, length 439 cm, Cx 0.24.

Gabbiano, Geneva 1983. Gull-wing coupé based on the Renault 11, length 390 cm.

Maya, Turin 1984. Preliminary sketch for a small saloon design with a centre-mounted V6 3 litre engine, 250 hp, financed by Ford. Length 421 cm.

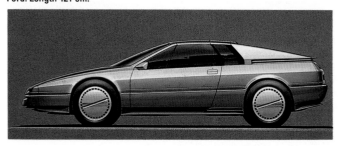

critical sessions in which designs are submitted for the opinion of potential customers and compared with the competition.

Unfortunately, in these tests, consumers tend to go for the least disconcerting solutions and forms which have already been accepted by public opinion. Such operations help to make marketing smoother but also stand in the way of innovation. They have sometimes proved costly for Giugiaro. But for many of his colleagues too . . .

A long-standing criticism of Giugiaro concerned his tendency to neglect aerodynamic considerations at a time when angular prototypes were his hallmark. The turning point in his career came with the Turin Motor Show: the simultaneous presentation of the Megagamma and the M8 mock-up threw new light on his work. The M8 was his first creation to go for aerodynamics, with a Cx of 0.24. Two years later, Giugiaro's mastery of this discipline was confirmed by the Medusa. This compact prototype took over the mechanical design of the Lancia Monte Carlo with its centrally mounted engine, offering a roomy passenger compartment with very advanced driving position. With its excellent aerodynamics (Cx 0.263) and its delicately sculpted form, the Medusa put paid to the cubist image established by Giugiaro's previous creations.

Ital Design confirmed this new departure with the Orca (Cx 0.245), a bulkier saloon built on a more conventional Lancia Delta base, then the Marlin (Cx 0.21) with a triangular profile reminiscent of the Audi 100, another car on which Giugiaro worked.

In 1986 the Incas featured a freer design; it was a smooth touring saloon using a centrally-mounted Oldsmobile engine. An aircraft-type control column replaced the traditional steering wheel. Japanese studies showed that young people were already familiar with this futuristic environment through video games.

All Giugiaro's creations are the embodiment of his own classical signature, his own academic approach. He has established a register of shapes which distinguish one generation of his work from the next. For the Lotus Etna, Giugiaro remained faithful

to the wedge shape of the Esprit, designed twelve years earlier, but just rounded off the angles.

Since 1978 Giugiaro has worked on other projects in parallel with his aerodynamic work; he has developed the hatchback concept that he launched in 1976 with the Alfa Romeo taxi which was developed at the request of the New York Museum of Modern Art. The Megagamma, the Capsula, the Together and the Asgard all showed just how far-sighted Giugiaro could be with functional vehicles.

With the Capsula, the key idea was to use a base comprising the engine, the mechanical components, the spare wheel and the luggage space. Any type of body could be fitted on top of this infrastructure. The Together had the same mechanical system as the Marlin. Still working along the same lines, the Asgard with its central engine offered one way of giving the hatchback a more noble look by applying sportier lines. The Orbit worked the same theme in a much smaller space (less than four metres long), using the same base as the Machimoto.

Taking the opposite line to the idea of function being more important than form, Giugiaro is putting his money on a revival of motoring for pleasure. With the hybrid Machimoto, his idea was to overcome the inertia paralysing the further development of cars. The Machimoto used a Golf GTI base, but the seats in this non-conformist sports car were replaced by two rows of saddles, providing room for six people to enjoy both the thrills of a motorbike (seating, open air) and the reassuring aspects of a car (stability, road holding). This type of realistic project shows that Giugiaro is perfectly capable of applying his flair to explore new horizons for cars. And when the constraints of the motor industry appear to have exhausted his imagination, Giugiaro pops up somewhere else, taking an unexpected road. The Aztec sports car, although more conventional than the Machimoto, nevertheless uses some unusual effects, such as the separate cockpits and the contoured head rests. Whatever he does, Giugiaro always pays the utmost attention to detail. The side panels were like magnificent high-tech sculptures housing dials, lights and electric plugs to check the vital

organs of the car.

Innovation in cars is a question of culture, which is why it has to be varied to match the social level of the designer's target market. According to Giugiaro, you can afford to be revolutionary at the lower end of the range, whereas the conservatism of the public sets the limits at the top of the range. Being sure of his ground on this point, and also being aware that it takes outside consultants to bring car manufacturers round to accepting revolution, Giugiaro managed to sell the Panda and the Uno to Fiat's top brass. With its rustic charm emphasised by flat windows, protruding hinges and washable interior fabric, the Panda was a clear departure from the tendency to flatter small-car owners by mimicking the comforts of large cars. It is taking

Opposite: <u>Lotus Etna,</u> Birmingham 1984. Prototype for a mid-engine small saloon, V8 4 litres, 350 hp. Length 427 cm.

Above: <u>Orbit,</u> Turin 1986. Mock-up for a compact hatchback saloon based on the VW Golf Syncro, length 398 cm, height 143 cm.

Below: Illustration signed "G. Giugiaro" for the Premier, launched at the 1987 Chicago Motor Show under the Renault banner then marketed by Chrysler.

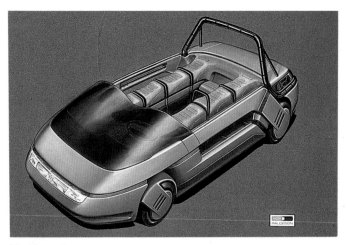

Machimoto, Turin 1986.
Hybrid vehicle based on
VW Golf GTI 16 V
mechanics. Length 398 cm.

this sort of stand, similar to the ones taken in the past with the Citroen 2 CV in 1948 and the Austin Mini in 1959, that Giugiaro has emerged as one of the great designers of his era.

Giugiaro's clientele has moved. He expressed all his fears in an interview given to the American weekly *Automotive News*: "As car manufacturers merge, so the number of our customers declines." Ital Design has done a lot of work with Japanese firms – Suzuki, Isuzu, Nissan and others – but he does not have any illusions about the openings in North America and Japan.

Incas, Turin 1986. Saloon with centrally-mounted Oldsmobile Quad 4 turbo engine, 4 cylinders, 2260 cc, 230 hp; developed from the Maya chassis, length 445 cm. Gull-wing front and back doors, aircraft-type driver's controls.

The Americans have a plethora of design teams and barely have any dealings with outside consultants, while the Japanese are managing to do without their European consultants nowadays. Giugiaro has found new openings in countries which are still lagging behind in design. Giugiaro was called to Spain by Seat for the Ibiza, he has worked for Hyundai of Korea since 1974 and Zastava of Yugoslavia asked him to design their Florida saloon.

Previous double page and above: <u>Asgard,</u> Turin 1988, luxury hatchback. length 441 cm, height 157 cm. Photographed in front of the old Fiat factory at Lingotto, now the venue for the Turin Motor Show.

Above: <u>Aspid</u>
Opposite and following double page: <u>Aztec,</u> Turin 1988; two designs on the same base with Audi 200 Turbo engine, 5 cylinders, 2.2 litres, 250 hp. Length 427 cm.

Le Corbusier's Voiture Maximum as seen by Ital Design for the centenary of the architect.

Giugiaro has lived through some crucial changes in the car industry. After a short spell at Fiat, he was in charge of styling at Bertone from 1959 to 1965 then at Ghia between 1965 and 1968 before going on to found Ital Design. Working from these vantage points, Giugiaro was able to see developments in car design – and his own limits – from afar. In 1970, Giugiaro created an "Industrial Design" department to handle all projects except cars. In 1981, this division became an independent company, "Giugiaro Design" headed by Giuliano Molineri. This outfit has its own team of stylists which has designed cameras for Nikon, watches for Seiko, electronic organs for Bontempi, a bus for Volvo, white goods for Candy and televisions for Sony, not forgetting "marille", a new type of pasta produced by Voiello! Since 1983, there has been a line of clothing bearing the "Giugiaro Uomo" label.

In 1987, Giugiaro made his contribution to the centenary of Le Corbusier by putting together a full-size wooden model of the Voiture Maximum designed by the architect in 1928. This was Giugiaro's act of homage to an esteemed predecessor who, like him, preached functionalism and a certain way of living. Giugiaro's success makes him a target for sniping; a certain amount of repetition in his styling and his strategic weaknesses have left him exposed to criticism. But for all that, Giugiaro is still one of the most disturbing and influential designers of his age.

**Remember these initials: I.DE.A. is a company in the process of turning the little world of Italian coachbuilding on its head. It appeared at the dawn of the Eighties with new ideas about car design.**

Above, Franco Mantegazza, Chairman of I.DE.A. and the Fiat Tipo. Opposite, the Ferrari Pace Car, made for PPG Industries (1987).

S omewhere in Moncalieri there is a turning on to a little road which winds along the side of a hill. The vegetation becomes thicker and thicker, hiding the sumptuous villas where the gentry of Turin live quietly. A dozen kilometres further on, as the forest becomes even thicker, is 32 via Ferrero de Cambiano: a forbidding gate, cameras peeking from the trees, maybe microphones too, and an entryphone. This is the entrance to a vast estate where the XVIII century villa Cantamerla is enthroned amongst the wisteria and cypress trees.

It was the presentation of the Fiat Tipo in March 1988 which brought I.DE.A. out of the shadows. A competition to design it brought projects from Ital Design, Centro Stile Fiat and I.DE.A., and it was I.DE.A. which won. The initials stand for Institute for Development in Automotive Engineering, founded in December 1978 by Franco Mantegazza. The personality of the man explains the particular nature of the house. Born in 1929, Franco Mantegazza claims to be pure Genoese. He started his studies in Milan, then went on to obtain a mechanical engineering degree from the University of Zurich. His career then took him from one country to another; he worked in Sweden, then in Germany (with Volkswagen), then he came back to Italy (with Magneti-Marelli), then he crossed the Atlantic to offer his services to VW of America before a spell in Morocco,

The Ferrari PPG Pace Car in the grounds of the villa Cantamerla, in Moncalieri.

Fiat VSS 1981. Project for a
car made up of "sub-
systems" designed by the
architect Renzo Piano, one
of the heads of I.DE.A.
between 1978 and 1981.

One of the preliminary
sketches for the Fiat Tipo.

Prestige saloon car project
for General Motors in 1981.

which has left him with some rather unusual turns of phrase
when he speaks French. Mantegazza made a foray into Fiat-
France during the Sixties before founding I.DE.A. – right in the
middle of the energy crisis, right in the middle of a time of
change in the motor industry when new faces were at a
premium.

Mantegazza's team breaks down as follows; Giancarlo
Cavazzuti is in charge of administration, Marzio Raveggi looks
after the commercial side and Marco Fantini takes care of engineering. On another site below villa Cantamerla are the construction workshops and the design offices. I.DE.A. brings
together a total of about 215 people. In charge of the design
department since 1983 has been Ercole Spada, a name well
known to lovers of Italian beauty. He was born in 1937 and
started his career as a stylist in 1960 at Zagato where he was
behind some of the coachbuilder's biggest successes. In 1969,
Spada set up on his own and then in 1970, he went into the
design studio which Ford had established in Turin before it was
incorporated into the Ghia studio. After a brief spell at Audi,
Spada then joined BMW in 1977. His right-hand man at
I.DE.A. is the polytechnic graduate Justin Norek, a colourful
character of Polish origin. There are about twenty stylists from a
variety of backgrounds working at I.DE.A., including François
Lampreia, a French stylist who worked for Citroën for seven
years and eight years with Renault before trying his hand
abroad.

What sets I.DE.A. apart from its rivals? For a start, there is
the personality of its chairman, who manages to be both effi-
cient and warm. Without being boastful, Mantegazza tries to
outline the originality of his business by taking his references
from the Bauhaus, by advocating the mutual enrichment of art
and technology and by maintaining close collaboration between
designers and engineers. The Institute has achieved its success
without any publicity and without making a splash at motor
shows. This has enabled I.DE.A. to adopt a different tone to
its competitors; it is not weighed down by years of tradition, nor
hemmed in by the constraints of a house style. When the Insti-

tute takes on a job for a major manufacturer, it does not put its own stamp on the job. With each job, the designers at the Institute do their utmost to go along with the manufacturer's brand image, not their own.

The outcome of this is that more and more people are turning to I.DE.A., such as the Fiat group in Italy. Then at the end of 1987 came the Ferrari small saloon car which was financed by PPG Industries and intended to become the pace car for several American races. Other names which beat a path to I.DE.A.'s door have been BMW from Germany, Volvo from Sweden and Chrysler and General Motors from the United States. But I.DE.A.'s activities are not confined to cars; Franco Mantegazza's interest in boats has led to collaboration with the Baglietto shipyard. Being a pragmatic outfit, I.DE.A. has applied its talents to all sectors of design (civil engineering, household goods, industrial vehicles, tools etc.).

I.DE.A.'s first project to be implemented in the car industry was the Fiat VSS in 1981, designed by the architect Renzo Piano; he was a co-founder of I.DE.A. and stayed with the firm until 1981. The VSS was a modular car featuring a reticulated structure providing on its own, the load-bearing function of the traditional monocoque while "sub-systems" took over the function of a skin.

There was very little talk of I.DE.A. in those days, but as time went by, its reputation spread. Mantegazza never misses an opportunity to pay his respects to the old hands of the design business: "They have been fantastic craftsmen," he says, meanwhile swearing that I.DE.A. will never design a new type of pasta. With his double-edged compliments, Franco Mantegazza seems to condemn all his rivals to the scrap heap. No doubt this faith in the future is one of his strongest cards.

The designer François Lampreia and the Ferrari/ PPG Pace Car; he created the interior styling.

Part of the team of stylists meeting with Justin Norek.

Project for PPG Industries.

**Ghia is the only Italian coachbuilder to have thrown in its lot with a major manufacturer – Ford. Their association confirms the influence of Italian design and its power to educate.**

Altair, Geneva 1980. Saloon based on the Ford Granada 2800, length 470 cm.

AC-Ghia, Geneva 1981, Small saloon car based on the AC-ME 3000, central engine, V6 3 litre, 138 hp, length 389 cm.

Ghia took off in the immediate post-war period with the arrival of a new boss, Mario Boano, in 1946 and a new young business manager, Luigi Segre, in 1950. These two men set about revitalising the old business founded by Giacinto Ghia in 1915. They quickly sensed that the Americans were becoming receptive to Italian know-how. The new wave of American designers were casting respectful looks towards a country which dared to throw out its aesthetic models and old methods and start again. Virgil Exner was one of that generation which turned its back on the excesses of Detroit. He trained during the Thirties at the "Art and Color Staff" of General Motors, spent some time in the studios of Raymond Loewy and then joined the Chrysler Corporation in 1950. The Americans and the Italians decided to get together and Chrysler and Ghia went on to form an idyllic relationship that was to last almost 15 years (from 1950 to 1963) until the departure of Virgil Exner. This long period of collaboration established the Ghia brand on the other side of the Atlantic.

In early 1973, Ford bought the minority shareholding which De Tomaso Inc. held in Ghia. It then created the Ghia Operations subsidiary headed by designer Filippo Sapino, who since 1970 had been in charge of Italian Design Studio, a little outfit which Ford had set up in Bruino in 1970. Sapino started his career as a designer with Ghia in 1960 at the age of 23 and spent only a brief period away from via Montefeltro when he went to work for Pininfarina between 1967 and 1969. Once Henry Ford had Ghia under his wing, he began to take on some of the Latin qualities which he dreamed of. With Ghia, his right-hand man Lee Iacocca managed to do what he had not managed with Ferrari several years earlier. For the Americans, Ghia became a stamp of European "good taste" and the badge

Pockar, Turin 1980. Small car based on the Ford Fiesta.

Shuttler, Brussels 1982. Compact (length 325 cm, wheel base 200 cm) and aerodynamic (Cx 0.32) saloon car on Ford Fiesta mechanical base.

Quick Silver, Geneva 1982. Five-seat saloon car with central V6 3 litre engine on the same chassis as the AC

extended by 29 cm (wheelbase 259 cm, length 456 cm) Cx 0.30.

Barchetta, Frankfurt 1983. Sports car based on the Ford Fiesta XR2, length 350 cm.

bearing the famous "G" proliferated on Fords the world over.

Using this label, Ford acquainted the great American public with a different feel and gauged its ability to accept innovation. Ford's financial muscle gave the coachbuilder the strength to build dozens of prototypes and to pursue investigations in all directions – in a spirit which was often more opportunistic than pioneering. Town cars and all-purpose vehicles, luxury limousines and sporty saloons were all tried.

The Eighties started with the Altair saloon, presented at the 1980 Geneva Motor Show. With its classic, angular saloon car profile, it still had one wheel safely in the previous decade. But Ghia set a new course in March 1982 with the Quick Silver, a fastback with soft, rounded lines with a central engine to give a good Cx (here too a 3 litre V6 taken from the Granada). Only two years separated these two cars, but during these two years cars moved into the age of aerodynamics. The difference is apparent in the rapid development seen in top-of-the-range saloons; in just two years, the Cx figure became an essential advertising factor.

The numerous Ghia prototypes shown at all the Motor Shows helped to prepare the public for the aerodynamic forms which Ford are adopting both in Europe and in North America. The rounded forms of the AC-Ghia, the Avant-Garde, the Shuttler and the Brezza were all precursors of production cars: the Sierra, the Scorpio and the Taurus. The compact, sporty Shuttler was based on Fiesta mechanics while the Brezza, designed by Marilena Corvasce, and the Avant-Garde, took the Escort as their starting point. These three cars claimed Cx figures of between 0.30 and 0.32. From the point of view of looks, without a doubt the most attractive is the AC-Ghia, a stocky small saloon based on the British AC ME 3000.

Other concepts loomed on the horizon of the 1980s and Ghia made sure they did not pass by untried. First there was the arrival of hatchback "minivans": the launch of the Aerostar in the United States in early 1985 was preceded by several Ghia designs, such as the Aerovan. Ghia went on to pursue the same line with the APV (Geneva 1984) and the Aerostar HFX (Frankfurt 1987).

Similarly, the launch of the Ford Taunus and Mercury Sable station wagons in 1985 was accompanied by several experimental estate cars designed by Ghia in order to give this type of coachwork a new image (Vignale TSX-4 in 1984 and TSX-6 in 1986). These showed that functionalism and a family character could be married to elegant and sporty looks.

Opposite: Cockpit, Geneva 1981. Three-wheeler mini car seating two people in tandem, Piaggio 200 cc engine. Length 328 cm.

Below: Trio, Geneva, 1983. Three-seater four-wheeler mini-car, two-cylinder 250 cc engine, length 241 cm.

Three designs, three styles for North America: the <u>APV</u> van (Geneva 11984) with a 1.6 litre engine, the <u>Vignale TSX-4</u> estate (Turin 1984) derived from the Ford Tempo and the <u>Lincoln Gilda Vignale</u> convertible (Paris 1986).

Below and opposite: <u>Saguaro</u>, Geneva 1988, compact all-purpose saloon, length 432 cm, Cx 0.29.

Ghia's penchant for town cars can be seen in three projects which came up with very different solutions. The distinctive feature of the Pockar was its luggage compartments in the doors; the two-seater Cockpit, with its Piaggio engine, harked back to the tandem seating position of the Messerschmitt bubble car; and finally the Trio was an ultralight and ultracompact little car seating three people in a triangular arrangement. Ghia acknowledged another trend from the Eighties, the return of sports cars, by creating the Barchetta. This car, based on Fiesta XR2 mechanics, was shown at the 1983 Frankfurt Motor Show and went on to provide the basis for the new Mercury Capri in 1988.

Ghia's Turin workshops are increasingly being used as an advanced platform for American styling centres. Sometimes Ghia is happy to put together mock-ups from plans provided by Detroit, such as the Lincoln Vignale Gilda, which was shown in Paris in 1986 and in Tokyo in 1987.

More original was the Sagauro saloon unveiled at the 1988 Geneva Motor Show. This compact car attempts to combine the features needed for town driving with the possibility of getting off the beaten track, thanks to substantial underbody protection. These features are contained in a rounded body very much in keeping with the aspirations of bio-design.

This is how Ghia responds to movements in styling while playing its role as Ford's bridgehead into Europe – not inspired, but certainly assiduous.

**Luckily for the Zagato brothers, good reputations are long on staying power. Their famous name was beginning to lose some of its sparkle until a British love affair and a Japanese contract put the spotlight back on to them.**

Car industry tongues started wagging in earnest when the Zagato brothers announced in March 1985 that they were pursuing a project with Aston Martin. Zagato! The name still inspired respect, their spirit was venerated, but there was no new product to bring the dream up to date. The Aston Martin Vantage Zagato may only have been dreamed up to put the old Milan factory back on to a modern track, although irrespective of motives, it bears all the marks of a legend: mystery, challenge and élitism. The entire output of the Vantage Zagato was voluntarily limited to 50 models and was delivered between March 1986, when the first prototype was presented, and the end of 1987. Fifty far-sighted enthusiasts actually signed cheques for £87,000 after seeing nothing more than a Giorgio Alisi sketch. Aston Martin and Zagato teamed up again in March 1987 to produce the Volante Zagato convertible, which was even more exclusive since the production run stopped at 25.

Like Bertone and Pininfarina, Zagato is first and foremost a dynasty currently headed by the brothers Elio and Gianni Zagato. Elio, born in 1921, is chairman of Zagato S.p.A.. At the factory he is affectionately known the "the pilot". Brother Gianni, the engineer, is eight years his junior and manages the commercial and industrial branch, 'Zagato Car s.r.l.' Miro Galuzzi is in charge of the "Zagato Industrial Design" department.

Elio and Gianni took over reins of the dynasty from their father, Ugo, who died on 31 October 1968. Ugo was not quite thirty when he founded "Zagato & Co." in via Francesco

Opposite: <u>Zeta 6</u>, Geneva 1983. 2 + 2 based on the Alfa Romeo GTV 6, 2.5 litre V6 engine, 160 hp.

Ferrer, Milan, in 1919. Initially Ugo Zagato worked for all the Italian manufacturers before he and Alfa Romeo established closer links based as much on affinity as on proximity. The 6C 1500 and 1750, then the 8C 2300 were destined to set the seal on the Alfa Romeo-Zagato association for posterity. At the end of the Thirties, Alfa turned to another major Milan coach-builder, Touring, which was in the process of developing the "Superleggera" [Superlight] technique. Zagato turned instead to Lancia.

## The coachbuilder of original and sporty designs

After the war, Zagato continued to use its technical expertise (especially in aerodynamics) in motor racing. However, style became an increasingly important element under the influence of Elio. In 1947, he created the "Panoramic" line which consisted of extending the glass surfaces upwards.

The brothers Elio and Gianni Zagato with the Aston Martin Vantage Zagato, presented at the 1986 Geneva Motor Show.

VANTAGE ZAGATO

Zagato has always been the firm for original and sporty designs. Bodies with the "Z" insignia produced in small numbers were the lightest and the most aerodynamic – in other words, the sportiest. Zagato gradually eased out of crafts and into industrialisation, moving into new premises in Terrazzano di Rho, a Milan suburb. In 1960 Zagato took on the stylist Ercole Spada who was to give the Zagato style an even more pronounced character. It was under him that the most memorable bodies appeared and the style became more innovative (cf. the Alfa Romeo Tubolare, the Aston Martin DB4 GTZ, the Lancia Fulvia and Flavia Sport). In 1970 he was replaced by Giuseppe Mittino, who was without a doubt less inventive and more inconsistent.

On the business front, Zagato's situation became alarming during the Seventies. After being dropped by Lancia in 1972 and by Alfa Romeo in 1975, Zagato had to find other ways of keeping the factory going. Little electric cars and bullet-proof bodies were very much in line with the vicissitudes of the times: the restrictions imposed by the oil crisis and the bloody escapades of the Red Brigades. Then came the Lancia Beta sports car and the Bristol 412. In 1983, creativity came to the fore again; at the Geneva Motor Show, Zagato unveiled the Zeta 6, based on the Alfa Romeo GTV 6. Mittino had managed to rediscover the sensual lines of the golden years and it was this prototype which prompted the directors of Aston Martin-Lagonda, Victor Gauntlett and Peter Livanos, to offer the Zagato brothers a new contract. In 1984, Maserati entrusted Zagato with production of its Biturbo sports model.

In 1987, Zagato reached an important deal with the Japanese company Autotech, a subsidiary of Nissan, which is going to produce a touring saloon designed by Zagato Industrial Design and built by Zagato Car. The firm may not be euphoric, but at least it is getting its confidence back. About one hundred employees mill around the beginnings of a production line where Maseratis will be assembled, painted and finished – the parts will be stamped out by outside subcontractors. The dozen people in the design studio have shaken off their depression and are looking to the future again. In his office, behind dozens of trophies, Elio Zagato allows himself the smile of a man who has remained true to his calling.

**Aston Martin Vantage Zagato**, Geneva 1986. This car, chassis number 20011L, is one of the earlier cars in a series limited to fifty. V8 engine, 5,341 cc, 432 hp.

**Aston Martin Volante Zagato**, Geneva 1987. Prototype of a convertible with a production run limited to 25.

The prototype of the
Volante Zagato was
disfigured by an unsightly
bulge on the bonnet, but the
use of fuel injection rather
than carburettors in
production models allowed
a flat bonnet to be used.

**Premature death left Edgardo Michelotti heir to a great name in Italian coachbuilding, but he responded to the challenge with great dignity.**

Edgardo Michelotti and Tateo Uchida. Below: Meera S, 1983. Opposite: Pac, Turin 1984. Small car based on Daihatsu Cuore mechanics.

Following double page: Pura, Turin 1986. Mid-engine sports car, Alfa Romeo turbo 1,779 cc, 155 hp, length 356 cm, AlbaTech chassis.

Giovanni Michelotti was just 58 when he was struck down with cancer on 23 January 1980, leaving his children Daniela and Edgardo and the helm of a firm of twenty people. On the creative side, the inheritance was taken over by Tateo Uchida, a Japanese stylist working in the firm since 1964. Giovanni Michelotti was one of the most prolific stylists of the post-war period. He started with Stabilimenti Farina at the age of 16 and broke loose in 1949 to become the darling of the coach-building world: Allemano, Ghia, Bertone and Vignale all called on his skills. Then manufacturers started clamouring for him and the fate of several – Triumph, Alpine and BMW – took a new turn, thanks to him. Giovanni Michelotti was the first coachbuilder to offer his services to the Japanese; the Prince Skyline Sport (1961) and the Hino Contessa Sprint (1962) were designed in Turin. When Edgardo Michelotti took over the business, he was faced with the problems of the economic crisis, but today balance has been restored. With his canny outlook, Tateo Uchida put together prototypes which have left their mark on history even if they did not anticipate it: the CVP39 (1981) large-capacity estate car based on the Fiat Ritmo [Strada in the UK] or the curvaceous CVT58 (1982) based on the Alfa Romeo. For several lucky customers Michelotti continued to produce one-offs such as a Ferrari 400i "Meera S" ordered by an Arab prince, and a Lola brought by an industrialist. Edgardo Michelotti had the good sense to develop the Far Eastern links established by his father. In Japan the badge adorns a multitude of objects. Moreover, Michelotti lured manufacturers by using Japanese mechanical systems for two designs: the Toyota Clas coupé (1986) and the Daihatsu Pac (1984), a city car with an original method of assembly. Then Michelotti added a new dimension to his company when he presented the Pura at the 1988 Turin Motor Show. Going beyond a mere study in style, he put together a structure which combined carbon fibre and aluminium, with the help of Mario Colucci, a former disciple of Carlo Abarth, and the AlbaTech Company. With ambitions of this order, Michelotti shows that small production runs can offer a way out for coachbuilders.

Marcello Gandini with his masterpiece, designed for Bertone: the Lamborghini Miura, built between 1966 and 1972.

# GANDINI

**In the world of style, there are some talents who make their name without becoming sensationally famous. One such name is Marcello Gandini. Today he is independent but he continues to be one of the most original figures of his time.**

Marcello Gandini is not known to the public at large, but among his peers he is regarded as one of the greatest stylists alive. This superlative also brings to mind Giorgetto Giugiaro, another giant of contemporary design. The comparison is inevitable but facile on closer consideration. To be sure, both men were born in 1938, the Chinese Year of the Tiger, and their paths crossed at Bertone. On the other hand, they are worlds apart in their philosophy of style and way of life. Coincidences of time and place are the main things they have in common, just as Schoenberg and Stravinsky lived in the same area of Hollywood without ever speaking a word to each other.

There is a long drive through the Susa valley to Almese. At the other end of the village is a steep track, a bend overgrown with brambles, a dry stone wall, another bend and an iron gate. Marcello Gandini's house is hidden behind a second wall which forms the back of one of the buildings. A little wooden door leading on to a patio is the way into his world.

# GANDINI

Marcello Gandini is proud to show off his surroundings, which are an indissoluble part of his personality. He savours the difference between the quality of life which he has achieved today compared with his early working years. He made his name with Bertone, joining them in 1965 to replace Giorgetto Giugiaro, who did not want to share the place with another stylist. He was to stay almost 15 years, establishing a real research department and setting a certain tone. Gandini transformed Bertone's research department. When they hired him, he was alone with a model-maker and stylist Pierre Stroppa, who would later be in charge of interior styling at Renault. He successfully pushed to have the styling centre moved to Caprie in the mountains, away from social upheavals. Having known the advantages and the disadvantages of life in a big company, Gandini decided that it was time to give his individuality free rein.

The Citroën BX and the Renault Super Cinq designed by Marcello Gandini and photographed in the courtyard of his home in Piedmont.

Mist veils the slopes of the hill, but the building retains the colours of the sun with red ochres and pinks and *trompe l'oeil* effects. Marcello Gandini has lived here since 1984, but for years he dreamed of this country house, built around 1630 on the remains of a previous building dating from the Middle Ages. Marcello Gandini spent a long time looking for a place like this, mellowed with age, no doubt with the intention of adding something of his own history to it.

Gandini constantly stresses that a technical grounding is an essential part of the stylist's job. Several years ago he designed a totally new car. The design relied on an assembly process in which 80% of operations were to be carried out by robots, doing away with the classic assembly line and thereby reducing the size of the factory. Régie Renault ended up buying the rights to the project . . . just to stop others getting hold of it. Gandini's knowledge of the technical side has helped him to gain the respect and the confidence of engineers, not to mention their indulgence. He is one of the few stylists who can alter schedules and challenge points which were regarded as established by architects.

A vast Renaissance tapestry adds a touch of drama to a space which mingles austerity and mannerism. There is something baroque about Marcello Gandini, in his penchant for high sophistication, in his fascination for American cars from the Fifties. And certain aspects of his work also reflect this; Gandini is very careful with his ornamentation. You just have to look at the Carabo and all its little wings which accentuate the animal quality already suggested by its colour and body panels, or the Citroën BX and the way the panels are worked, so typical of this period when Bertone was playing with lines and angles like nobody else.

Gandini's family background was not in plastic arts but rather in music. His father was a pianist and composer. His pieces are still played occasionally, but few people remember his name. Marcello identifies strongly with this idea of living out a passion in secret.

Night changes the mood of the courtyard and throws a different light on the car bodies. The workshop is laid out in the fourth side of the internal courtyard. One wall is all glass, the other is white; the only decoration is a corner chimney from a bygone age. This is where Marcello Gandini works. This is where, in 1986, he outlined the first sketches of a replacement for the Lamborghini Countach.

RENAULT 5 TSE

TO · 58297D

He starts by quickly roughing out any ideas which he has had during the night. The fleeting ideas flow from the tip of his pencil before specific contours are outlined in a 1:1 scale drawing. As is usual with great coachbuilders, the car is drawn on a large scale which is then sent out to sub-contractors to be translated into a mock-up.

Marcello Gandini is a loyal collaborator and a tenacious enemy. His favoured customers are still Renault and Citroën in France and BMW in Germany. With Renault, Gandini actually had an exclusive contract for several years which resulted in the Renault Super Cinq and the interior styling of the 25.

Manufacturers who call on Gandini's skills expect an approach which breaks the confines of the normal. They are looking for an avant-garde type, someone provocative, a creative spirit with enough confidence to swim against the current, and a man who never does the same thing twice. People accept whatever he does; they know that he is capable of going off schedule and overturning a programme. Anyway, Gandini is never really competing with other stylists. He is somewhere else, above the ebb and flow of fashion. Technicians accept him and marketing men dread him.

This austere and baroque, individualistic and warm technician lives like an artist; he is a modernist with roots that go deep into the past. A secretive and paradoxical man, he can afford the luxury of making his reputation behind a veil of discretion.

The Countach S was produced almost up to the 1990s. It has something in common with the geometrical lines of this baroque octagon.

**He is one of the few designers to have taken the plunge and gone independent. This lonely road has led him from extravagance to pragmatism.**

The Modulo, based on the Ferrari 512 S, designed by Paolo Martin in 1968 when he was working for Pininfarina.

Gobbi, Turin 1984. Country car based on the Fiat Panda 4x4, built by the coachbuilder Maggiora.

Designer Paolo Martin is easily spotted among his peers as his physical appearance does not match his profession. He is a shy, stooping man with a rather careless appearance. In other words, it is not fashion plate looks but rather his original talent which have brought him to prominence. He was born in 1943 and has followed a tortuous path through the most fertile areas of Italian coachwork. He started his career in 1961, learning design, modelling and panel work with Giovanni Michelotti. He then spent a few months with Bertone and in 1967 took charge of styling at Pininfarina. He was involved in every project until 1972 and in particular, put his signature to the extraordinary Modulo, one of the most personal creations of the era. Martin went on to work for Ghia, Moto-Guzzi and Benelli and then spread his wings in May 1976. Since then he has been refining his taste for functional vehicles. At his first public appearance at the 1984 Turin Motor Show, he presented the Spazio 3, a three-wheeler utility vehicle, and the Gobbi, a very countrified Panda; both cars were built by the coachbuilder Maggiora. At the 1985 Frankfurt Motor Show, he presented the Halley coupé based on the Fiat Uno and characterised by the design of its windows. Martin used the occasion of a trade fair held in Shanghai in July 1985, to put forward a design for a very simple modular vehicle. The "Modular Civil Tractor" was based on a standardised chassis on to which could be fitted a variety of bodies to carry goods or people. The idea was taken up in 1988 in the Freely prototype which was built by the Savio coachworks: the chassis, using the mechanical design of the Fiat Panda 4x4, can be fitted with a hardtop for the road but a quick stop is all it takes to put up a canvas top to shelter two people.

With this line of research, Martin is emphasising how it is possible to serve both the need for motor vehicles in the Third World and the demand for new leisure vehicles in developed countries.

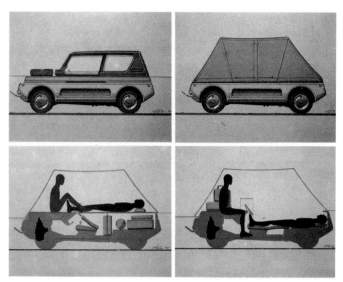

Freely, Turin 1988. Modular
vehicle based on Fiat Panda
4x4 built by Savio
coachworks.

**Anybody who sees cars as more than just a way of getting from A to B has dreamed of building their own. As the Twentieth Century draws to a close, some privileged people are pursuing their dream.**

Luigi Chinetti Jr. in front of his first sketches and the model of his convertible based on the Ferrari 365 GT 2 + 2.

Below and preceding double page: from "model" to working prototype – a dream made real.

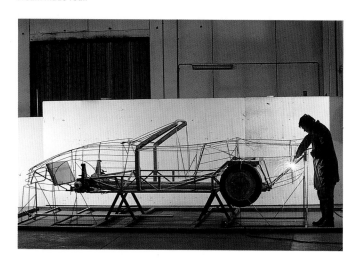

L uigi Chinetti Jr.'s piece of good luck came early in life in the shape of his father Luigi Chinetti Sr., three times winner of the 24-Hour Le Mans: in 1932 and 1934 in an Alfa Romeo and in 1949 in a Ferrari. Chinetti Sr. became a legendary personality as he took the Ferrari myth to the four corners of the world. He won America over to the cult of the Prancing Horse by taking those thoroughbreds across the Atlantic, racing them under the banner of the NART (North American Racing Team) and putting young bloods behind the wheel (the Rodriguez brothers, for instance). Milanese by birth, Luigi Chinetti is as well known for his hot temper as for his stubbornness, whereas his son has the smiling approach of a dilettante. Being brought up in this world soon gave him the urge to create Ferraris of his own. So the Chinettis, father and son, had coachworks build several special Ferraris to their specifications. Chinetti Jr., known to some people as "Coco" turned a prototype 275 P into a small saloon and designed an estate car based on a Daytona; the former was built by Michelotti in 1969 and the latter was put together by Panther in Great Britain in 1975. The passion is still there. In 1987, he dreamed up a body to put on to a shortened and reinforced 365 GT 2+2 chassis. The body was built in aluminium by Bachelli & Vila coachworks following the great tradition of Modena. This unpretentious creation is just a foretaste of other, more substantial dreams. The proof of this is that Luigi Chinetti Jr. has left the comfort of North America to return to the magical atmosphere of Emilia.

**Under the baton of a redoubtable conductor, the Fiat group has turned design into the driving force behind its commercial revolution and industrial reconstruction.**

Autobianchi/Lancia Y 10 Geneva 1985. Production model designed by Centro Stile Fiat.

The Fire 1000 engine fitted in the Autobianchi Y 10 in 1985 was styled by Rodolfo Bonetto.

For the last 10 years, Mario Maioli has held sway over the ante-rooms of the Fiat group. His official title is "style coordinator", but what he actually does is much more ambiguous. A graduate of Milan Polytechnic School, this devilish Lombard trained as an architect. He drew up the plans for airports in Genoa and Kampala, and for a Turin underground railway system which came to nothing, before coming into the Fiat empire in 1973; his job was to clear the plots for the factories in the south. Four years later in the styling department at Lancia, he had to call on his skill as a diplomat in asking Pininfarina to redesign the radiator for the Delta – bearing Giugiaro's signature! Since then, Maioli has been smoothing relations between independent designers and the in-house stylists, coordinating their work and liaising with the upper echelons. Some are under contract for many years. The couturier Ermenegildo Zegna has a hand in researching and supplying cloth (for Lancia and Ferrari), his colleague Missoni is a valuable colour consultant, interior styling specialist Rodolfo Bonetto has designed a number of dashboards for Fiat and Autobianchi and the Veglia-Borletti dashboard instruments for Ferrari. He was also the one who "designed" the Fire 1000, the first engine to be "styled". And of course we must not forget Ital Design who put their name to the Fiat Panda, Uno and Croma and the Lancia Delta, Prisma and Thema. But what has become of Centro Stile Fiat itself, overshadowed by Maioli? Very few of its designs have come to anything apart from the Autobianchi Y 10. In October 1986 Ermanno Cressoni replaced Gian Paolo Boano in the job into which Mario Boano, his father (a former Ghia man and also a coachbuilder) had steered him by setting up Centro Stile in 1957. Ermanno Cressoni is a renegade from Alfa Romeo, where he was in charge of styling at the time when the controversial lines of the Alfa 33 and 75 were laid down. On the fringes of the styling centre since 1986, Robert Opron (formerly of Citroën and Renault) has been running a small team looking more towards the future and discovering new talent.

Maioli never lets routines or schemes get established – an approach which is proved valid when his daring bets come off. When it came to making the definitive choice for the Fiat Tipo, it was I.D.E.A. which won the contract. Once again, Maioli was not entirely unconnected with this about-turn. No doubt the emphasis put on the passenger compartment in the design of the Tipo awoke his architect's instincts . . .

**Turin is to cars what Milan is to fashion and interior design – a capital, a star pulsing with creativity.**

Ipotesi, Turin 1982. The Fiat Ritmo [Strada] as seen by Aldo Sessano (Open Design).

Rayton Fissore Magnum, 1984. Luxury off-road estate car produced in small numbers, designed by Tom Tjaarda, Iveco chassis, Fiat, Sofim, Alfa Romeo or BMW engine.

Italy has had only one major motor manufacturer since Alfa Romeo joined the Fiat group in January 1987. This monopoly has created a dangerous situation for the galaxy of businesses which are arrayed round Turin, round the almighty Fiat. This development in the local economy comes on top of far-reaching transformations which are affecting the world of design. Openings for independent studios have become fewer or moved in response to the new industrial groupings, in accordance with Fiat's new line-up. The Japanese, who used to be very good customers, have matured to the extent that they can increasingly manage without the Italians. Design studios have to prospect for new customers in still unexplored economic areas. Another worrying factor is the development of design training round the world. Right or wrong, top colleges enjoy a level of prestige which manufacturers find reassuring. They can build up their teams with young stylists cast in the international mould and avoid calling in outside consultants.

Nevertheless, Turin continues to exert a powerful pull in the world of coachbuilding. The nature of sub-contractors has changed over the decades. In bygone times, they were coachbuilders who divided their time between creating and manufacturing, but these craftsmen were unable to keep up with the times and wandered off into re-fitting, armour plating and other utility conversions. Moretti, Savio, Boneschi and a few others are still surviving thanks to these mundane requirements. The role of coachworks has been taken over by design studios. Many are run by former "integrated stylists" who have broken away, such as Tom Tjaarda, born in the United States in 1934 with a lot to live up to since his father, John Tjaarda, designed the Lincoln Zephyr just before the boy was born. Tom Tjaarda emigrated to Italy to take up with Ghia in 1959, Pininfarina in 1961, Ghia again in 1967, Fiat in 1978 and finally Rayton Fissore in 1981. It was under this banner that he dreamed up the Saab Viking coupé, the Seat Ronda, several designs for Chrysler and the off-road Magnum before starting up his own company, Dimensione Design, in November 1984. Mike Robinson, another American, also came to try his luck in Turin in 1981. Emmanuele Nicosia left Pininfarina to found Design System at the end of 1985. Eurodesign brings together

Dashboard designed by
Mario Bellini for the Lancia
Beta, updated in September
1978.

Maggiora AC-4WD, Turin
1988. Design for an off-road
vehicle built on a shortened
Fiat Ducato chassis,
designed by Eurodesign
and manufactured by
Maggiora.

the Frenchman Joel Brétécher (another old hand from Pininfarina) and the Italian Aldo Garnero. Open Design has been going since 1977 under Aldo Sessano, who went independent in 1968 and is very much orientated towards Japan, where he works with Mitsubishi. For other great designers such as Mario Bellini or Rodolfo Bonetto, cars are just another object for industrial design, which makes their contribution to Fiat's interior styling all the more valuable. The list of designers who have settled in Turin could go on and leads one to the conclusion that very few of their colleagues have set up their drawing boards outside Piedmont. Still, it is worth mentioning Domenico Nardiello (ex Alfa) in Milan, Francesco Bonielo in Padua and Pierangelo Andreani together with Jorge Arcuri at "A System" in Milan. Adreani was a stylist at Fiat, Pininfarina and De Tomaso, for whom he designed the Maserati Biturbo before throwing over the traces in 1981. With so many designers emerging, model builders sprang up. Sergio Coggiola has been set up since 1966 and is one of the most established. Manufacturers and coachworks can also get a hand from firms like "G Studio", which has been working in the Susa valley since 1960, or the Per Car company, run by journalist Giancarlo Perini since 1983.

Teaching and communication are also part of the "Turin effect". The School of Applied Art and Design has become one of the most reputable in Italy. The magazine *Auto & Design*, under the guidance of the respected journalist Fulvio Cinti, provides lively and well-documented information for all professionals in the field of design.

Turin is still a magical town. Even though it is shrouded by the mists of the river Po and its palaces are darkened by layers of dirt, it still retains its charm. The old Piedmont houses manage to hide the monstrosities of the Mussolini era in much the same way as the hills manage to hide the dreadful factories in the lowlands. Turin continues to be the capital for car bodies. Detroit or Los Angeles might well be forging the designers of the future, Tokyo might well be capable of putting together oriental dreams and Paris, Stuttgart and Coventry might well be stiffening their ranks with stylists, but Turin is still there with its own specific character, and still acts as a counterweight to Milan, capital of *interior* design.

We are seeing a change in the art of Italian coachwork. Some institutions are having a hard time while other new strengths are emerging. As long as culture continues to be more important than computerised robotic intelligence, Turin will remain a crucible for the art of coachbuilding.

Distancing itself from the harsh reality of the economic crisis, the United States began to dream. Young designers were carried along by a worldwide learning process and started changing their world – no doubt with the idea of preparing for the American Revolution.

**''America is neither a dream nor reality; it is hyperreality. It is hyperreality because since the very beginning, it has lived as Utopia Achieved. Everything here is real, pragmatic, allowing you to dream.''**

Ford Probe IV, January 1983. Four-door four-seater saloon, front-mounted 1.6 litre 4-cylinder engine, length 475 cm, Cx 0.15.

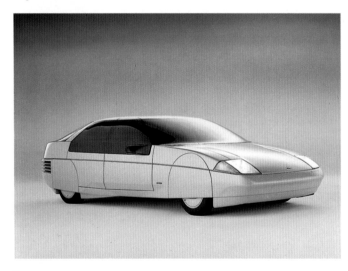

Ford Probe V, Tokyo, October 1985. Two-door 2+2 coupé, central engine, 4 cylinders, 1.9 litres, 185 hp, length 487 cm, Cx 0.13.

These words by Jean Baudrillard seem appropriate when you look at American industry through the dream cars which have left their mark on the automotive culture of this country. Unlike Europe, the United States makes no distinction between ''culture'' and ''automotive culture''. Cars have no place in European culture, which has other historical roots to draw on, whereas on the other side of the Atlantic, cars are a key part of history, a key feature of the ''American Way of Life'' and its socio-cultural outlook. Europeans who worship cars turn them into a ''passion''. Americans even celebrate their banality (cf. pop art or hyper-realism). Europe is still stuck with a left-over of the 1920s when intellectuals and artists could decide whether to be fascinated or disgusted by ''machines'' freeing man while subjugating him. In the United States, nobody questions cars because they are an answer to everything. Thanks to the freeways which breathe life into the whole country, cars have even helped to paint a picture on the canvas of the desert.

So what is a dream car in this empire where extraordinary things become part of the commonplace, where dreams are no more than a blip in reality? American dreams do not have the utopian, inaccessible value felt in Europe. They are not an antidote to reality, but rather a premonition of it. Dream cars are there to give people a taste of their own future . . . and of their own power. Because this filigree work is a vision of America triumphant. High-tech references are never given for the purpose of giving a name to some unlikely mutant, but rather to go into the melting pot of U.S. technology.

Motor Shows are a time of dream and reality; present and future combine to form a continuum of sound and light. When the curtain falls, the dream ends. The message from American show cars is not aesthetic. They are not dedicated to eternity (with a view to creating *objets d'art*) but rather destined for obsolescence. Reality is consummated and dreams are consumed. Dreams on one side of the Atlantic do not have the same meaning as on the other. American society is founded on the very idea of putting into practice what others have only dreamed about. American dream cars have to be seen from this standpoint.

Contemporary styling bears vigorous witness to the great leap forward made by American industry during the last fifteen years. Today the American perception of the car calls on new values:

– humility (in the considerable reduction of the outside dimensions of so-called standard models)

– modern techniques (adopting the universal layout of front wheel drive, using V6 engines instead of some of the larger V8 engines and using less old-fashioned suspension),

– purity of line (becoming aware of aerodynamics: this brings to mind the "streamlining" of the Thirties, as if waking up from an economic crisis – 1929 and 1979 – always involved finding purified, reassuring lines),

– austerity (with the gradual disappearance of decorative frills, chromework and jutting fenders).

Ford MSSX-1, 1986: model of a four-door saloon car with central engine, built by Ghia stylists.

Ford Bronco DM-1, Detroit, January 1988. Compact all-purpose vehicle (length 424 cm) designed by Derek Millsap as part of a programme for the Art Center College of Design of Pasadena, financed by Ford.

Lincoln Machete, Detroit, January 1988. Four-seater coupé with "switchable privacy glass" enabling glass to be darkened.

ASC Vision, 1985 saloon powered by Chrysler 2.2 litre 4-cylinder turbo engine, 146 hp, length 432.

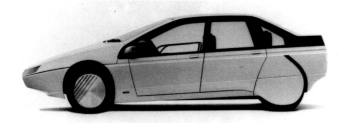

American cars have obeyed these four commandments and radically changed their appearance. By rejecting the opulent look, cars have dropped their social status. Until then they had symbolised, rather naively, the arrogance of a whole race. Each era had a way of expressing this: the Fifties full of chrome and fins, the Seventies with their angular, overprotective forms (a period of safety thinking spread by Ralph Nader). It was paradoxical that a nation should express its strength in such prosaic ways while finding itself bogged down abroad in Vietnam and torn apart with racial conflict at home.

## "Aero-design"

Nothing remains of those chrome and steel fantasy objects. The Ford group was the first to practise the lessons of the American automobile revolution by introducing more rounded, lighter lines. The Thunderbird started the ball rolling in September 1982, followed by the Ford Tempo and the Mercury Topaz in February 1983, then the Ford Taurus and the Mercury Sable in the spring of 1985. Behind the scenes of these mass production cars, Ford hammered away at promoting "Aero-design", developing the "Probe" family of prototypes. Cx figures fell consistently. The Probe IV saloon recorded a Cx of 0.15 in 1983, then the Probe V presented at the 1985 Tokyo Motor Show grabbed the record with a Cx figure of 0.137, even though it was a fully-operational vehicle carrying three people.

In 1980, Donald F. Kopka took over from Gene Bordinat (1920-1987) as head of the Ford Design Centre. But the real craftsman behind the "Aero-design" movement was Jack Telnack, in charge of North American Design in Dearborn until he succeeded Donald Kopka on 1 June 1987. Clearly this refined style helped towards Ford's increased sales. However, this does not mean that America's second-biggest manufacturer is neglecting other possibilities. The Bronco DM-1 4x4 Compact shown at the Detroit and Geneva Motor Shows in 1988 is an interesting variation on the all-purpose theme. Apart from this, Lincoln is grooming its brand image; the Vignale Gilda, built by Ghia in 1986, and the Machete coupé, shown at the 1988 Detroit Motor Show, confirm just how conservative this company is.

Styling also played a key role in the corporate recovery of

Chrysler Portofino,
Frankfurt 1987. Saloon with
centrally-mounted
Lamborghini engine, V8 3.5
litres: model built by
Coggiola in Turin.

Plymouth Slingshot, Los
Angeles, January 1988. Fun
car with centrally-mounted
2.2 litre , 16-valve
turbocharged engine.
Length 378 cm.

Chrysler. When Lee Iacocca picked up the reins of the group in November 1978, Chrysler cars were too old-fashioned. Having encouraged the birth of the Mustang at Ford in 1964, Iacocca knew full well that design was one of the prime factors of success. The first sign of renewal was the launch of the Dodge Caravan and Plymouth Voyager minivans in 1983. Then came the generation of H-Cars (Chrysler Le Baron GTS and Dodge Lancer) introduced in 1985. The lines were more flowing yet still rather reserved, but the nettle had been grasped. In 1983, Chrysler set up a styling department in Carlsbad, California. The Chrysler Pacifica department was headed by Don DeLa Rossa, an ex Ford man like Iacocca. When DeLa Rossa retired in June 1986, he was succeeded by Tom Tremont. Unlike the Design Center in Highland Park, Michigan, Chrysler Pacifica's brief is to look to the future. It has come up with several promising designs. Worth mentioning are the Dodge Mohave shown at the Vancouver Expo 1986 and again in Los Angeles in 1988 under the name of Daytona X91: the Plymouth Slingshot, a little fun car with a very lively character, and the Dodge Intrepid. However, the prototype which was most highly regarded in Europe was the Chrysler Portofino, a saloon with four gull-wing doors; it was built by Coggiola in Turin, fitted with a centrally-mounted Lamborghini Jalpa engine and unveiled at the 1987 Frankfurt Motor Show.

The Americans are very shy of Europe and rarely take the trouble to show the fruits of their creativity away from home. An exception to this tendency is ASC, the only American outfit comparable with Ital Design or I.DE.A. Originally in 1965, the American Sunroof Company did just what its name suggests; since then, the name has been changed to American Specialty Company and it employs a thousand people involved in a variety of activities. Manufacturers come to consult ASC about turning their cars into convertibles (Saab for the 900, Porsche for the 944, Buick for the Reatta etc.) Now ASC has a design studio with five stylists; it produced the "Vision" prototype in 1985.

The existence of schools such as the Art Center College of Design in Pasadena, or the Center for Creative Studies in Detroit has transformed the face of design both in America and worldwide. These places go back a long way; the CCS was the successor to the Art School of the Detroit Society of Arts and Crafts, founded in 1906. As for the Art Center, it first opened its doors in 1930. These schools provide a high level of teaching which is reassuring for the major automobile manufacturers.

Just as American design was entering its Renaissance, fate played a cruel trick by striking down one of its most colourful figures, Raymond Loewy (1893-1988). Throughout his life he advocated a purification of American design. Apparently his modern day heirs have understood that ugliness just does not sell.

**In 1986, Chuck Jordan became the fourth man to have presided over the fate of design at General Motors. Now Jordan is laying down the outlines of 21st century America – with a lot of punch.**

Lean Machine, 1983. Single-seat three-wheeler with fixed rear end and articulated front end for motorbike-style cornering. 185 cc Honda ATV engine. Shown at the Disney World Epcot Center.

Chevrolet Aero 2000, 1982. First prototype of a series of aerodynamic vehicles, Cx 0.23. It was followed by the Aero 2002 in 1982 (Cx 0.14), the Citation IV in 1983 (Cx 0.18 with front-mounted V6 engine) and the Aero 2003 in 1986 (Cx 0.16, also front-mounted 2.8 litre V6 engine).

Going into the GM Design building is like entering a time warp; it seems as if nothing has changed since Harley Earl left in 1958. There is the same huge old office inlaid with light oak designed by Earl himself, the same furniture with its typically Fifties "modern" lines, the same bay windows with one side opening on to the rectangular lake with a water tower redolent of old comic books and the other side looking on to the dome of a "sci-fi" type auditorium. This is the heart of the GM Technical Center, a town within the town of Warren, which itself is one of the population centres which make up the urban sprawl of Detroit. No indeed, nothing of this functional decor has changed since it was designed by the Finnish architect Eero Saarinen in 1956. The future of America still ferments within the GM Design Building.

The man in charge of design since 1 October 1986 is one Charles Morell "Chuck" Jordan, successor to three powerful personalities whose charisma still pervades the atmosphere. Americans do not refer to their past as a source of nostalgic romanticism, but rather as a nourishing memory worthy of respect and a reassurance of their future strength and ability. Chuck Jordan takes just a few sentences to sketch out a portrait of his predecessors and at the same time, to point the main sequence of events in fifty years of history. In 1927 Harley Earl created the "Art & Color" department at General Motors, thereby setting up the very first styling department to operate inside a car factory.

Buick Wildcat, 1985. Small saloon designed from an original sketch by David P. Rand. Centrally-mounted 3.6 litre V6 engine, 230 hp. It won the 1985 Car Design Award.

Chevrolet Corvette Indy, Chicago. Small saloon car with centrally-mounted V8 2.65 litre 600 hp engine derived from an Indianapolis block. Four-wheel drive, four-wheel steering, active suspension. Styling by Jerry Palmer, the man behind the Corvette '84 (illustrations by Serge Bellu).

95

**Chevrolet Express,** May 1987. AGT-5 Turbine car, capable of carrying four people at 240 kph to compete with aircraft over short distances. Cx 0.195.

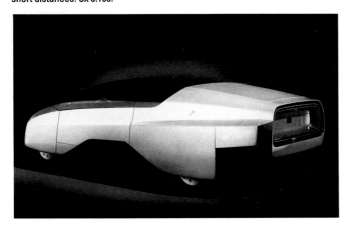

**Chevrolet Ventura,** New York, January 1988. Saloon car for the near future, in the same category as the

Chevrolet Corsica. Front-wheel drive, 3.1 litre V6 engine.

This extraordinary, Hollywood-type figure dictated General Motors style for more than thirty years through the landmarks of modern U.S. history, from Roosevelt's New Deal through to the prosperous Eisenhower era. His flamboyant style incorporated these changes, resulting in the tail fins of the '59 Caddy – a superb display of vulgarity. However, this outlook meant that Harley Earl was falling behind designers such as Loewy, Teague, Bel Geddes and Dreyfuss, and never took part in the crusade for purer "streamlining". However, Bill Mitchell succeeded him in 1958 and did take part in the changes in automobile styling. Art & Color first became GM Styling and then in 1972 re-emerged as GM Design Staff. Mitchell was the first one to assimilate the lessons of Italian coachwork to any meaningful degree, preferring a sculptural rather than ornamental approach. Irvin Rybicki held the job from 1977 to 1986, a period of bleak soul-searching for the U.S. automobile industry. This dour man never became a "star" in the mould of his two predecessors, but it was under his guidance that cars underwent their most radical changes.

## The return of the Dream

A new era began with Chuck Jordan, born in California on 27 October 1927. He studied at MIT (Massachusets Institute of Technology) and joined General Motors in 1949. In 1957 he was put in charge of Cadillac styling for five years, when he replaced Clare McKichan as head of Opel. Today Chuck Jordan has around 1,300 people under him, about a third of whom are creative staff. Working alongside vice-president Jordan are two executive directors: David Holls for design and K.A. Pickering for engineering. The design staff is made of 36 studios divided into seven departments: CPC (Chevrolet/Pontiac/Canada/Saturn), BOC (Buick/Oldsmobile/Cadillac), trucks, advanced design, advanced concepts, colours & materials and international coordination. The latter department looks after work carried out by Opel, Vauxhall, Holden, Isuzu, Suzuki and subsidiaries and partners of General Motors.

Pontiac Trans Sport,
Chicago 1986. One-piece
body with 2.9 litre V6 turbo
engine, front-wheel drive.
Wheelbase 295 cm, height
151 cm. Styled under the
direction of Terry Henline.

The company's modern products (Chevrolet Beretta, Astro, Camaro, Corvette, Pontiac Fiero, Buick Reatta, Cadillac Seville and Oldsmobile Toronado) are all the results of a far-reaching revolution and prove that General Motors is far in advance of its rivals in terms of styling. The future of General Motors has now been set by prototypes unveiled over the last few years. The Aero 2000 set the scene for a whole generation of aerodynamic show cars. The Buick Wildcat (1984), the Chevrolet Corvette Indy (1986), the Oldsmobile Aerotech (1986) and the Pontiac Pursuit (1987) have successfully delved into the resources offered by "animal" forms, using the subtleties of bionics for both the interplay of exterior volumes and the lay-out of interiors. In January 1988, GM recreated the spirit of the Motoramas of the 1950 in an exhibition intitled GM "Teamwork and Technology for Today and Tomorrow". The same baroque setting of the Waldorf Astoria in New York also housed a series of prototypes – Pontiac Banshee, Chevrolet Venture, Cadillac Voyage, Buick Lucerne and GMC Centaur – each of which was intended to clarify the image of each division of the group. An insight into their longer-term research can be obtain from a look at the more radical Pontiac Trans Sport a one-piece minivan (1986), the Chevrolet Blazer XT-1 (1987) fun car or the Chevrolet Express (1987), designed to compete with aircraft over short distances. The Express was designed by the advanced styling centre at Newbury Park, established in California since 1983 as the Advanced Concepts Center.

"Cars take on a different look under Californian skies," says Californian Chuck. With his determination, cars might end up taking on a whole lot of different aspects right across America . . .

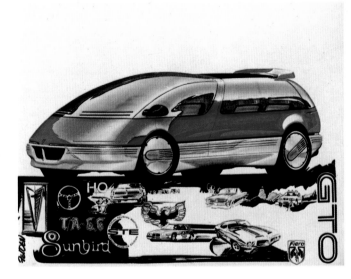

Pontiac Pursuit. January
1987. Four-seater with
front-mounted engine, 2
litres, 200 hp, four-wheel
drive, four-wheel steering.

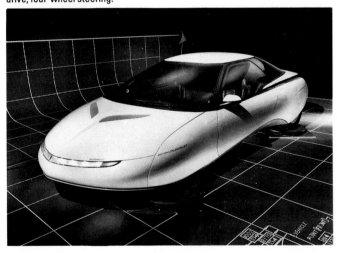

Oldsmobile Aerotech,
September 1986. Single-
seater saloon on March
Indy chassis. "Quad 4"
engine, four cylinders, 2.3
litres, 16 valves. Carbon
fibre body, length 488 cm. It
took several world speed
records in August 1987 on
the Fort Stockton track in
Texas; with driver AJ Foyt it
clocked up 430 kph on the
flying mile.

W ith so many cars bearing the mark of the Italian coachbuilders, it is about time the French car industry settled its disputes with French design. Are cars missing out on the pulses stimulating industrial creativity in France?

Below: Project for driver's position by Michel Harmand, 1980 and Karin project by Trevor Fiore. Gull-wing coupé, three seater with driver in the middle, length 370 cm, height 107 cm.

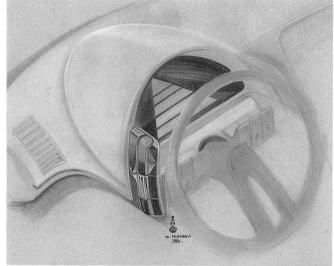

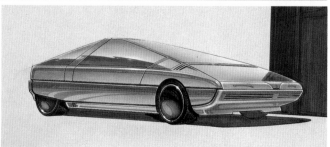

Above: Xenia, Frankfurt 1981. Mock-up for a hatchback saloon car, length 420 cm, height 123 cm. On show at the National Car Museum in Mulhouse.

**"This is humanised art, and it may well be that the DS [Déesse = Goddess] marks a change in the mythology of cars. Until now, superlative cars tended to be powerful beasts; with the DS, they became both more spiritual and more objective."**

Activa, Paris 1988. Working prototype, four-wheel drive, four-wheel steering,

"managed" suspension, engine WM V6, 3 litre, 220 hp, length 475 cm, Cx 0.25.

Eco 2000 Paris 1984. Prototype economy car. Final version "SA 109";

three-cylinder 749 cc engine, 35 hp, length 349 cm, 480 kg. Cx 0.21.

This was how Roland Barthes celebrated the advent of the Citroën DS in France. A dynamic piece of sculpture, the pinnacle of Citroën style, its very weight is still making waves in the turbulent history of the double chevron. Citroën cars have always been the stuff of legend. The 2CV, the *Traction* and the DS are part of French folklore, part of its cultural and social heritage. The last 2CV came off *french* production lines in February 1988. It started out as a farm hand and ended up as a jack-of-all-trades after satisfying post-war populism, cradling 1968 student revolutionary passions and pacifying ecologists before ending up in the hands of well-bred young ladies.

After the death of Flaminio Bertoni, the genius who moulded every Citroën from the Traction onwards, Robert Opron set about the task with a mixture of panache and humility. But one day in 1975, Opron left to set up Renault's styling centre. For several years Citroën had no guidance in its styling, which was entrusted to the obscure care of the research department, which led to the awful Visa. The BX was saved from a similar fate by Bertone, but everybody at Vélizy knew that it was time to set up a proper styling centre with a proper boss.

Trevor Fiore was appointed to this job in 1980. A wandering stylist born in 1937, his Franco-Italian origins and British education combined to form a cosmopolitan personality. He learned the technical side at Standard-Triumph and then discovered industrial aesthetics with Raymond Loewy. Fiore went independent in 1964 and collaborated for a while with Fissore coachworks, designed the TVR Trident and the Elva-BMW, then worked for Monteverdi, Alpine, Daf, Aston Martin, Gilbern, AC, Coggiola and De Tomaso. He became a full-time consultant with Citroën on 1 January 1980 and six months later was taken into the research department. Trevor Fiore lost no time at all in getting the go-ahead to build the Karin, a show

car presented at the 1980 Paris Motor Show. The Karin's pyramid shape and futuristic interior with the driver in the middle were intended solely to show that a new Citroën style was being created. The hatchback Xenia unveiled at the 1981 Frankfurt Motor Show was intended to be more realistic.

The man in charge of the research department, Xavier Karcher (who was due to become vice-president/director-general in 1988) played a part in the renaissance of Citroën style. Here is a man who knew the importance of design; he forged close relations with the Art Centre College of Design and took care to put out European feelers in Vevey. Several young stylists were put on courses in California, including Jean-Claude Bouvier (born 1953) and Eric de Pauw (born 1949). Jean-Claude Bouvier made his mark in 1984 when he thought up the Dromos, a development vehicle articulated like a pair of compasses, and the Citron, a candidate to replace the 2CV. As for

Eric de Pauw, he designed a small competition car in 1981. Leaving aside the up-and-coming generation, we turn to Michel Harmand, one of the most outstanding personalities of the "old guard", who continued to look after the Citroën brand image for a long time. Hired in 1964, he took charge of the Interiors Design group in 1976. He is a shy man who has always been bold. He was the man behind the half-moon dashboard of the CX and the control "satellites" around the steering wheel (Visa, GSA, BX etc.). Harmand graduated in Fine Arts with painting, then in Decorative Arts with interior design, and has always looked for solutions which avoid stultifying automatic responses. By transforming the motorist's world, he has established a sensual and sensuous relationship between men and machines.

The style centre moved on in 1982. Being something of a dabbler and an artist, Trevor Fiore was not up to running a

Eole, Geneva 1985.
Prototype of a saloon car based on the mechanics of the CX. Entirely machined by computer. Length 477 cm.

the 1983 Decorative Artists Show.

The little unit in Sophia Antipolis soon shut down to leave the field clear for the new "advanced styling" PSA set up in Carrières-sous-Poissy under the management of Arthur Blakeslee. From 1975 this ambitious American had been running the Chrysler studios at Whitley near Coventry, where the last Sunbeams, Simcas and Talbots were produced. Blakeslee shipped Anglo-Saxon men and methods to Carrières. It was this team which put together the ECO 2000 programme presented at the 1986 Paris Motor Show; the PSA research and scientific affairs department was also involved, because the objective was to reduce fuel consumption to three litres per hundred kilometres, equivalent to about 93 miles per gallon. Three prototypes were built (SA 103, 117 and 109) between 1982 and 1984 and the Cx figure was finally reduced to 0.212. The process which led up to the construction of the Eole is not so straightforward. This ungraceful prototype was designed by Jeff Matthews and shown at the 1985 Geneva Motor Show.

Carl Olsen was ousted in April 1987 and replaced by Arthur Blakeslee, who lost no time in replacing Michel Harmand with Robert Matthews, while his namesake Jeff Matthews lasted only a few more weeks in his job. Olsen went back to the United States to take on important teaching duties in Detroit (Director of "Transportation Design" at Ford & Earl Associates and the the Center for Creative Studies). Harmand found refuge with Peugeot. Continuous management coups and the American dominance have produced a feeling of unease. Designers are trying to meet up again within the Peugeot group and even inside the Vélizy research unit. All this instability has played right into the hands of Bertone, who has become a valued partner. Let's hope that in future, the powerful Citroën legacy will enable the company to rediscover its individuality. The Activa prototype augurs well for such hopes.

rigid structure. He was "moved" to the South of France to set up a small unit researching "advanced styling" on the site of Sophia Antipolis. Meanwhile in Vélizy, "applied styling" was put in the hands of Carl Olsen. The new man was born in the United States in August 1934 and graduated from the Pratt Institute in New York; he went on to work for General Motors, returned to his parents' native Denmark in 1961 and then spent the period from 1963 to 1972 with Ogle in England, while teaching at the Royal College of Art. Spurred on by this new boss, the Vélizy Styling Centre was reorganised into five groups: Exterior Styling (11 designers headed by Jeff Matthews), Interior Styling (five stylists under Michel Harmand), the prototype production workshop, the "feasibility" department (seven people) and Colours & Decoration (four people). To celebrate the creation of the latter team under David Robillard, the colour specialist Roselyne de Mennedeu did a special job on a BX for

**It seems strange to talk about a "Renault Style" in view of the disparate selection of men who have shaped it and the way in which they have practised their art. But amidst all its diversity, Renault is often in the vanguard of design.**

Operating prototypes tested out at Montlhéry in October 1983. <u>Eve Plus</u>, 50 hp 1595 turbo-diesel engine, 168.8 kph, Cx 0.225

<u>Vesta 1</u>, three-cylinder 718 cc 32.7 hp engine, length 327 cm, weight 510 kg, Cx 0.25.

<u>Vesta 2</u>, June 1983, prototype of an economy car, fuel consumption reduced to 2.05 litres per 100 kilometres (about 135 mpg) at an average 90 kph,

2.73 litres (102 mpg) at 1220 kph. Three cylinder, 716 cc engine, 27 hp, length 354 cm, weight 473 kg, speed 140 kph. Cx 0.186.

his was the situation which Gaston Juchet found when he joined Régie Renault in 1958; within the research unit managed by Fernand Picard there was a coachwork department manned by Robert Barthaud and two stylists. Philippe Charbonneaux took this department over in 1960 and Gaston Juchet became his assistant in November shortly after his thirtieth birthday. This former student of the École Centrale, trained at Nord-Aviation, was to add a new dimension and set a new tone. From the moment he took up his duties, he began to hire stylists of the calibre of Béligond, Louis and Boué; he had a hand in the design of the revolutionary Renault 16 and gave his backing to the project which would later result in the Renault 5.

A new man appeared on the scene at Renault in 1975. Robert Opron was a trained architect and had gained styling experience with Simca, then with Citroën. He restructured Renault's styling centre by dividing it into two studios: applied style was put in the hands of Gaston Juchet while advanced styling was entrusted to Opron's faithful lieutenant Jacques Nocher. Styling continued to maintain its independence from the technical side and Bernard Hanon, who was appointed managing director of Renault in December 1981, backed Robert Opron's line on this. Many designers from outside the car industry were recruited: Olivier Mourgue, Mario Bellini, Marc Held and Terence Conran were consulted, painter Philippe Morisson came up with some new colour schemes for the interiors and the designer-colour specialist Jean-Philippe Lenclos laid the basis of the Colours & Materials sector. Pierre Dreyfus, by creating an Art & Industry section, had already made an opening to allow artists such as Soto, Dubuffet and Vasarely to have a hand in decorating the company's headquarters at Boulogne-Billancourt.

Renault's American foray had an impact on several products. In January 1979, the company signed an agreement with American Motors; this led to the production of the Renault 9, which was simultaneously launched in France and the United States in June 1982. This world-wide spread of activities meant that conventional shapes had to be made to match the tastes of every customer group. The confrontation between in-house stylists and outside consultants became increasingly heated. Marcello Gandini left Bertone and signed an exclusive contract with Renault. On other fronts, in 1981 collaboration with the manufacturer Teilhol produced the very inventive "Rodeo" designed by Michel Vlay, while work with Matra resulted in the Espace hitting the market in 1984.

The 1979 oil crisis put new priorities at the top of the agenda. In June of that year, the Agency for Energy Saving (later renamed the Agency for Energy Expertise) encouraged manufacturers to carry out research in this field and provided finance for it. That year, Renault designed the EVE prototype (*Eléments pour une Voiture Économe* – elements for an economy car), a car with all the chunkiness of the Renault 18. By the time it reached the operating stage, its Cx had been reduced to 0.239. Then in 1982 came the Vesta, a compact car of about the same size as the Renault 5. Six prototypes were built: three Vesta 1 and three Vesta Plus. In 1987 the developed version, the Vesta 2, achieved spectacular fuel economy records (2.8 litres/100 km – just under 100 mpg). The importance of aerodynamics in production cars also became crucial and the Renault 25 boasted a Cx of 0.30.

After Robert Opron had been ousted in mid-1984, Gaston Juchet stepped into the spotlight with Jacques Nocher at his side. By this time, the Styling Centre was divided into four departments: two separate studios for exterior styling, headed by Jean-Franois Venet and Michel Jardin, interior styling managed by Piero Stroppa and a "diversification" sector run by Jean-Paul Manceau to handle non-car business (industrial and farm vehicles, machines, under-bonnet styling. It was Manceau's team which was responsible for the decidedly "clean" look of the 2 litre Turbo 21 engine. Georges Besse, the new boss at Renault, decreed that tighter budgets were one of the key conditions for success. Nevertheless, intensive cooperation with independent designers continued. At the end of 1987, Gaston Juchet handed over to Patrick Le Quément, formerly with Ford and Volkswagen, and Renault began a new era at the threshold of the 1990s.

The Mégane was the company's first act of faith.

Mégane, Paris 1988. Prototype with four-wheel steering, V6 turbo engine, 3 litres, 250 hp, Cx 0.21, "clever" suspension.

Rafale, 1978. One of the sketches for the 129 project which eventually led to the Renault 25.

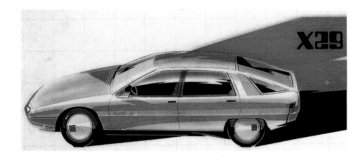

Renault 21, 2 litre Turbo, June 1987. "Styled" engine. 4 cylinders, 1995 cc, 175 hp.

**The walls of the old factory in Sochaux are trembling again. Over the last ten years, Peugeot's brand image has taken wing, largely thanks to Styling.**

G érard Welter and Paul Bracq are the unusual duo heading the Peugeot Styling Centre in the Paris suburb of La Garenne-Colombes. Paul Bracq is an old acquaintance. After attending Boulle college, he learned his styling with Philippe Charbonneaux in the early Fifties. It was the lottery of national service which brought him to Germany, which was to become the scene for crucial stages in his career. He polished his styling skills

Between 1957 and 1966 at Mercedes-Benz in the shadow of Karl Wilfert. he also met Alice, his wife and most fervent admirer. Paul Bracq returned to France for a brief stay at Brissoneau & Lotz before returning to Germany to head BMW styling between 1969 and 1974, designing the memorable 1972 BMW Turbo.

But Bracq was feeling more and more homesick and in 1974, at the age of 41, he accepted an offer to become joint director of Peugeot styling alongside Gérard Welter. The two men have nothing in common. Walter cultivates the image of a saturnine, shy and secretive stylist whereas Bracq, ten years his senior, is a voluble advocate of his profession.

Quasar, Paris 1984. Sports car built on the mechanical basis of the 205 Turbo 16. Centrally-mounted 4-cylinder 1775 cc turbo engine 200hp, four-wheel drive.

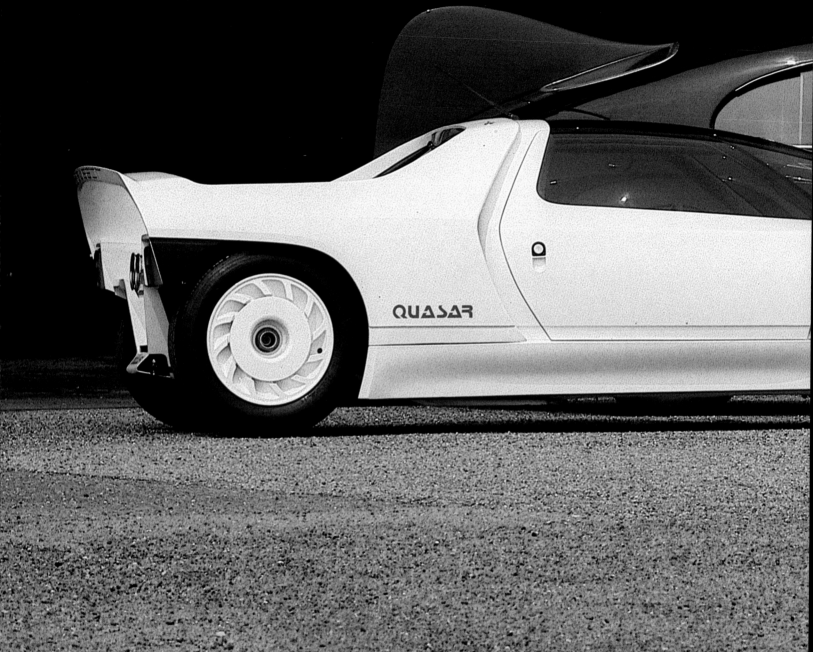

On Sundays their paths draw even closer together. Since 1969, Gérard Welter and Michel Meunier have spent their free time running the WM company producing competition prototypes which, thanks to its great tenacity, has managed to upset much better equipped outfits. Every year, WM rises to accept the amateurs' challenge of the 24 Hour Le Mans. In 1988, one of them broke the symbolic 403 kph on the Hunaudières straight. While Welter is getting oil stains on his overalls, Paul Bracq is adding to the paint stains on his; his paintbrush sweeps across broad canvases as the cars of his dreams emerge from the thick oil paint. So it's laurel wreaths for one, varnish for the other and champagne for all as art and sport are strangely united on Sundays. Then on Mondays they are back in the grey confines of La Garenne with their teams: exterior styling for Welter, interior styling for Bracq (the team was strengthened by the arrival of Michel Harmand in 1987). The PSA group has three styling studios: Peugeot in La Garenne, Citroën in Vélizy and PSA Advanced Styling in Carrières-sous-Poissy. A whole range of changes are under way in the workings of this outfit, which is equally likely to work on Peugeot and Citroën programmes. The departure of head man Blakeslee was followed by the arrival of Kurt Gwin, another Anglo-Saxon; Yves Dubernard and Jean Cavaud remained in their posts as assistants. Peugeot's style is inseparable from Pininfarina, their partner since 1955. It was this partnership which came up with the brilliant 205 and 405, and the company's optimistic mood was of course confirmed by the triumphs of the 205 Turbo 16, the world rally champion in 1985 and 1986. Success on the track and in the showroom has restored confidence within a group which was rocked to its core by the social and financial upheavals which followed the take-over of Citroën and Chrysler-France.

This feeling was reflected in the prototypes unveiled at Motor Shows. In 1982, Peugeot came up with the Vera Plus, a very serious saloon which met the demands of the Agency for Energy Expertise. Two years later, the scene changed after Peugeot had launched the 205, a "hot little number" which completely changed the mood of the old company. Flushed with new-found enthusiasm, the company invited stylists to give free rein to their imagination, first with the Quasar in 1984, then with the Proxima in 1986 and the Oxia in 1988. With unbridled imagination, Welter, Bracq and their colleagues have rediscovered the essence of extravagant show cars which flaunt their mechanical parts shamelessly and are not afraid of extraterrestrial forms and sharp contrasts. But beneath the gleaming metal and chrome innards of the Quasar, you can still make out the world champion 205 engine; the features of the 405 are implicit in the compressed lines of the Oxia. Message received. The dream is over but it remains in the collective memory as an image – a brand image.

**Oxia,** Paris 1988. Working prototype, four-wheel drive, four-wheel steering, central transverse V6 engine, 2.85 litres, four cams, 24 valves, 680 hp twin turbo, length 461 cm, width 202 cm, Cx 0.32.

Opposite and following double page: Proxima, Paris 1986. 22 coup, Kevlar body, central V6 engine, turbo, 2.85 litres, 600 hp, length 442 cm.

**Vera Plus,** 1982. Sketch for an economical mid-range saloon, direct injection 1769 cc diesel engine, length 419 cm, Cx 0.22. In 1983 developed into the Vera Profil.

**Matra Automobile is just a very small part of an enormous industrial machine, but the very fact that it is outside the company's mainstream activities gives operational flexibility and freedom to create.**

Above: <u>Project P 16,</u> one of the mock-ups of a hatchback van built on the mechanical structure of the Talbot Horizon.

Below: <u>Project P 29,</u> playful, aerodynamic and aeronautical.

Compared with Matra's aerospace, armaments and telecommunications interests, its automobile branch looks a real lightweight. But Matra plays the role of a fast and effective pioneer unit, able to advance along the side roads leading to the automotive future. Matra and Simca were linked in an agreement dated December 1969 which was taken over by the PSA group when it absorbed Chrysler-France in 1978. Unfortunately, with hindsight it has become evident that neither Chrysler nor Simca really benefitted from this move, but this was not for want of putting some interesting projects together. One in particular deserves a special mention. One Friday evening in 1979 Matra's technical director Philippe Guédon asked his stylist Antoine Volanis to put his mind to designing a leisure car to take the place of the Rancho, which itself was a one-off. The design had to be ready to show to chairman Jean-Luc Lagardère the following Monday. It took Volanis just a few hours to sketch the outlines of a hatchback vehicle inspired by American vans, which had graduated from being plain utility vehicles to become recreational runabouts. The bosses liked the idea and gave the go-ahead for the programme (under the code number P16, P17 and P18) and the building of mock-ups in early 1980. However, Peugeot backed away from the risk and dropped the project. So Matra turned to Renault in the autumn of 1981 and their partnership gave birth to the first one-piece saloon car in the world: the Renault Espace.

For the trade press, Philippe Guédon was "Man of the Year 1987"; for Matra, he is the man of the decade. He trained as an engineer at the Arts and Professions college and cut his teeth with Simca before starting his ascent of the ladder at Matra in 1963, where he became managing director in 1983. His outspokenness matches his dynamism. Ideas abound in the

Matra P 29, Sports car prototype using a wide range of composite materials. Transverse centrally-mounted engine, 1995 cc, 16 valves, 255 hp, length 410 cm, weight 840 kg. Standing beside the mock-up: Philippe Guédon.

research unit but Matra keeps its research to itself. The P 31 economy vehicle is still confidential; on the other hand, at the 1986 Paris Motor Show the public was allowed to admire the P29 designed by Aimé Saugues, Antoine Volanis' successor. The P29 looks like a cross between a buggy and a helicopter. It's fun, but the style is perhaps too impulsive to give a true reflection of Matra's skills.

**Since the death of the great French *Carrossiers*, the succession is open. Heuliez was one of the pretenders, but this old House has missed several opportunities.**

Opposite page: <u>Spyder Atlantic,</u> Paris 1986. Project based on the Peugeot 205.

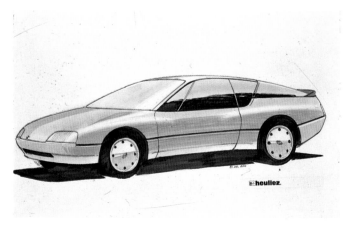

Above: sketch of the <u>Renault Alpine V6 GT,</u> GTA, shown in January 1985.

Below: Sketch for a prototype large capacity estate car shown in October 1988.

FRANCE DESIGN.

In 1922, a modest little forge was toiling away quietly in Cerizay, a village in Deux-Sèvres nestling in a dip in the low, rolling hills. Louis Heuliez had just taken over the family business making handcarts. Today, his grandson Jean-Pierre Heuliez and Gérard Quéveau are in charge of a group of two thousand people.

The younger generation did not want to get stuck with making cattle trucks and hearses, so they looked for new directions and nurtured a secret ambition to become the French answer to Bertone or Pininfarina, combining design and production. In the early 1970s, Heuliez started producing bodies for the Citroën M35 and specialised in production runs which were too marginal for the major manufacturers to carry out themselves. This led to involvement in sporting forays, with Heuliez taking part in the design and production of the Renault 5 Turbo, the Peugeot 205 Turbo 16 and the Citroën BX 4TC. With its excellent craftsmen, this coachworks produced prestige limousines based on the Peugeot 604 and the Renault 25, not to mention other less glittering products which are essential for the survival of coachworks. However, life in a research unit is equally precarious. A VW-Porsche designed by T.G.V. stylist Jacques Cooper in 1970 gave the first indication of Heuliez's desires on the styling front. After the arrival of Yves Dubernard the following year a studio was set up, but the real research centre was established at Le Pin in 1978. There were promising signs during these years of growth. Dubernard had a worthwhile group of stylists, among whom Gérard Godfroy and Patrice Sarrazin were the stars and Heuliez's efforts were repaid by the success of their projects, notably the Alpine GTA. Dubernard's departure from Heuliez in 1984 triggered an exodus from the creative studio, DEA turned into "France Design" and made a splash at the 1986 Paris Motor Show with the Spyder Atlantic. Back to square one. Heuliez has to win over customers among the major manufacturers, even though its styling centre is depleted, and come up with new industrial products. The company is still trying to find its way forward.

Preliminary sketch for
Matra P16, 1979.

Below: design for a
compact car for
Volkswagen, 1985, "Safari"
and "GT" free studies, 1988.

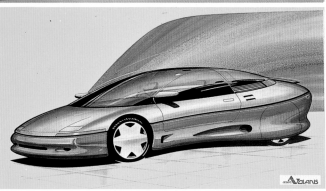

Antoine Volanis was far from a newcomer when he first came into the public eye at the 1983 Geneva Motor Show with his Hélios saloon. Volanis was born in Greece in 1948 but came to France at the age of five. He took a solid technical background to his first job at Renault before jumping into the big time at Peugeot; however, it was with Matra that he blossomed, being in charge of styling between 1971 and 1980. Under the guidance of Philippe Gudon, he became involved in exciting projects, designing the Murena and dreaming up the concept of what was to become the Renault Espace. Then Volanis felt that it was time to go it alone and set up his own business in November 1980. He was thinking big, imagining large premises housing a model workshop and a creative studio, just like an Italian coachworks. The one-piece Hélios was followed at the 1984 Paris Motor Show by the Apollon Saloon, which was credited with a record Cx of 0.13 and an S.Cx of 0.246. It looked as if Volanis was on the road to success. Volanis and his 10 colleagues had a workshop which earned its living by building mock-ups for PSA and Renault. Then things began to get sticky; Renault tightened the amounts budgeted for subcontracting, thereby leaving Heuliez in the lurch, sending Chapron to the wall and forcing Volanis to redeploy, meaning that he was forced to shut up shop and fall back on his design unit. He also had to diversify since the car industry was leaving him too little leeway. Antoine Volanis has since undertaken projects for Peugeot, Seat and Volkswagen, but at the same time he has scored successes in several new markets: a tennis racket for Donnay, a bathroom for Porcher, ski bindings for Look and the interior lay-out of the ATR 72 for Aérospatiale. Volanis still has several car projects up his sleeve; in early 1988 he went on an exploratory trip to Korea and Japan, making a lot of contacts in the process. Among the business cards which he brought back will be found the names of his future clients.

**The case of Antoine Volanis is a good example; it shows the difficulties of the design business in France and the hazards of freelance work.**

Following double page:
<u>Hélios,</u> Geneva 1983.
Compact one-piece with four separate seats, length 394 cm, height 150 cm. Cx 0.22.

Above and below: <u>Apollon,</u> Paris 1984. Saloon car built on a Renault 11 Turbo chassis. Length 455 cm, Cx 0.13. Antoine Volanis and his car, shown at the National Car Museum in Mulhouse.

119

"What could be more necessary than design when we want to export our products in the face of international competition?"

Triolet, 1988. Project advanced by François Quirin (F.I.D.) as part of a design competition organised by the magazine 'Automobiles Classiques'.

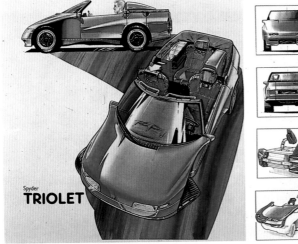

Arbracam, Paris 1988. "The last earth vehicle" dreamed up by students at the École National Supérieure de

Création Industrielle. Centrally-mounted Fiat FIRE 1000 engine, length 298 cm, 155 kph.

This is the question asked by Jack Lang, who already had the beginnings of an answer up his sleeve. Lang was Delegate Minister of Culture between 1981 and 1986, resuming the post in 1988, and has implemented a variety of initiatives to give design a real boost. The first step was to set up an Agency to promote industrial creativity; its task was to make business people, administrations and local authorities more aware of a discipline which was little appreciated in France. The public at large became familiar with a previously unknown breed of innovators; Philippe Starck, Andrée Putman and Pascal Morgue all came out of obscurity. Their work has become accessible through the major channels of distribution (Habitat, Le Printemps, Trois Suisses) and they have become media figures, thanks to orders from the State and to the national furniture competition. They have moved out of the closed world of insiders and into the street. In 1987, the Cartier Foundation gave Andrée Putman the task of setting up the *Hommage à Ferrari* in Jouy-en-Josas. At the Decorative Artists Show, consumers were finally able to touch the objects which both underlined their station in life and met the needs of their lifestyle.

The establishment of a Prize for Industrial Creativity has made it possible to honour disciplines such as fashion, design and comic books which were previously snubbed by the traditional Fine Arts. Education has been through a fundamental change; the École National Supérieure de Création Industrielle was set up in Paris in 1982. Under the auspices of its Principal Anne-Marie Boutin and encouraged by Citroën stylist Jean-Claude Bouvier, the "car studio" at the institute put together the Arbracam project for the 1986 Paris Motor Show. Throughout the country, education has enjoyed the benefits flowing from a dynamic resurgence of industrial creativity. In the various regions there are a dozen art schools now running design courses, not forgetting Compiègne University of Technology. In Paris there are two other public institutes teaching design apart from ENSCI: decorative arts (ENSAD) and applied arts (ENSAA), while the main private schools are ESDI, Ecole Camendo and ESAG.

But despite all these good intentions, there are numerous feuds and misunderstandings in the small world of industrial creativity. There are clashes of temperament between car styl-

MVS Venturi, June 1986. Small saloon produced in limited numbers by Manufacture de Voitures de Sport in Cholet from an original design by Gérard Godfroy. Centrally-mounted Renault V6 turbo engine, 2.4 litres, 200 hp, length 409 cm, weight 1280 kg, speed 240 kph.

ing and industrial design, as if one were intent on gobbling up the other. The new wave of designers features personalities such as Jean-Pierre Vitrac and Alain Carré who have been doing good business since 1970 and totally ignore cars. The most famous figures of the previous generation were unwilling to become involved; Roger Tallon, who invented the Minimax modular car in 1974, and Jean-Louis Barrault, creator of the Méhari, have limited their contributions to isolated projects. On the other hand, Louis Lepoix, who was one of the first to open a design studio, FTL, in 1950, has gradually become estranged from a largely uncomprehending automobile industry. Independent car stylists are becoming increasingly rare. Many of them dream of seeing their concepts turned into reality, following the example of Gérard Godfroy, father of the MVS Venturi, or Thierry de Montcorgé, the brains behind several off-road prototypes. However, looking abroad is sometimes the only way out: for Joël Brétécher, founder of Stirling Design in Nantes, the only way in which he could increase his field of action was to join forces with the Italians in Eurodesign. François Quirin and his team in *Formes industrielles design* have adopted a pluralistic approach; FID made its mark in various branches of industry both in Europe and in Japan. Now it has shown its intention to get into cars by linking up with Chausson industrial coachbuilders in 1987 to conquer South-east Asia. Robert Kohler of Kohler + Rekow studios is also expecting overtures from the car industry.

The last decade has without doubt been a turning point. Industrialists and the authorities have woken up to French design, and it is now being recognised. This statement has to be qualified when it comes to the car industry, but it is highly likely that there is a French *avant-garde* blossoming behind the school walls.

Volvo 260 by Hermès. Built by André Lecoq coachworks, one of the greatest specialists in the field of restoring collectors' cars.

Jules, by Thierry de Montcorgé, Paris-Dakar 1984. Six-wheel prototype, centrally-mounted Chevrolet V8 engine, 360 hp, polyester body.

# ATELIER 3D COULEUR

**Atelier 3D Couleur is located in an unbelievably charming old district of Paris, and it is there that Jean-Philippe Lenclos exercises the rare and *precious* profession of designer-colourist.**

Jean-Philippe Lenclos, designer-colourist, at his Atelier 3D Couleur.

Colours are a matter of geography and palettes vary from one country to another, from one region to another. Families of colours correspond to the behaviour of social groupings, to social or religious habits and to natural reflexes. The soft light of temperate climates tends to bring out coordinated tones, while colder countries go for contrasting colours. This "geography of colour" has been highlighted by Jean-Philippe Lenclos, founder of Atelier 3D Couleur in 1977. he first became aware of it in Japan, where vermillion-lacquered temples and multicoloured kimonos formed startling contrasts. The way in which colours harmonise is based as much on physical geography as on human geography. Climate, light and the geology of a place have just as much influence as skin colour in the composition of a palette. When Jean-Philippe Lenclos returned to France in 1965 after two years in Japan, the "new towns" springing up gave him the chance to put his observations into practice. Cars are also subject to the same colour considerations, but in their own complex way. The nature of the passenger compartment is very ambivalent, since it is both a very private place and at the same time very open to the outside world. Therefore drivers express their own personality in their choice of colours, materials and textures, but they do so with a certain amount of restraint. The reference points for cars include fashion, architecture and decoration, and Atelier 3D Couleur brings into play the interaction between all these disciplines. The colourist's job is to give his interpretation of how to combine poetic expression with technical discipline and the taste for novelty with respect for tradition. He must reconstruct messages from the past while interpreting the promises of the future.

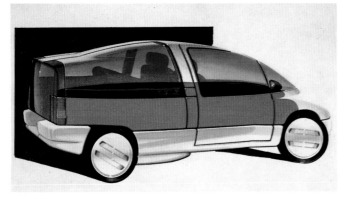

Ogle Design Project 2000, March 1984. Proposal for a compact family saloon. Mock-up presented at the 1984 Birmingham Motor Show, Cx 0.27.

G reat Britain suffers from the tradition syndrome. Its creative studios are sometimes haunted by the awkward ghosts of conservatism. But some *avant-garde* designers are exorcising them with the spirit of modernity.

Aston Martin Bulldog, Los Angeles, 1980. Small saloon with centrally-mounted engine, V8 5.3 litres tubo, multitubular chassis, length 472 cm. Built from a design by William Towns, also creator of the Aston Martin DBS (1967), Lagonda (1976) and the Hustler (1978).

Tradition is a two-edged sword which works to your advantage when it is acts as a rearguard for modernity; however, it works against you when it becomes an excuse for inertia. England relies on its tradition, fair enough. Nobody objects to the fragrance of Connolly leather, the burr of walnut veneer and the sparkle of hand-beaten aluminium, but these signals from history can only be picked up if they are put to the service of creativity. The decline of the British car industry is due in no small part to this nostalgic attachment to the past.

Jaguar is a case in point. Reinvigorated by privatisation and encouraged by its return to pole positions in competitive events, Jaguar set off again full of optimism. Unfortunately the XJ40 programme which gave birth to the new XJ6 series in 1986 was in its infancy during a period of crisis. The stylists in Coventry first consulted three Italian coachworks (Bertone, Pininfarina and Ital Design) but regressed to small-mindedness, as if paralysed by the beauty of the 1968 XJ6 saloon, due for replacement. As far as styling goes, Jaguar has been better structured since 1984; Jeff Lawson was put in charge and a studio was set up in the ultramodern premises formerly occupied by Talbot. The same reticence bogs down Rolls-Royce in conformity; the engineer in charge of styling, Fritz Feller, is a prisoner of its reactionary image, as proved by the Silver Sprite/Bentley Mulsanne range launched in 1980.

Aston Martin escaped from this slow slide into obsolete gentility, thanks to the powerful personality of the designer William Towns. The new generation launched in late 1988 confirms this dynamism, with a pair of young stylists from IAD, Ken Greenley and John Hefferman. Lotus shows the same urge to promote British design; in 1986 it organised a styling centre under designer Peter Stevens. He was formerly with the Ogle company, an independent outfit formed in 1954 and directed by Tom Karen; the company is still very active in industrial vehicles while pursuing its studies with cars.

London boasts one of the world's most reputable schools, the Royal College of Art, the scene of developments on the design front; its "Automotive Design Unit" was replaced by the "Department of Transport Design" in 1985. Nowadays, Britain's salvation is exporting its know-how.

**Don't hypocrites often have a tendency to justify conservatism by claiming the virtues of tradition?**

**Lotus Eminence,** September 1984. Prestige saloon design by Harris Mann, formerly designer with British Leyland and designer of the "Zanda" prototype (1969) and the Triumph TR 7 (1975)

**Jaguar XJ40** One of the preliminary sketches for the XJ6 saloon presented in October 1986.

**The Rolls-Royce** range as redefined in October 1980 with the launch of the Silver Sprite and the Silver Spur.

# I . A . D .

**In the space of about ten years, International Automotive Design has become one of the few design studios capable of holding its own against Italian coachworks.**

Hunter, Turin 1988. All-terrain vehicle derived from the Impact prototype.

Arrival Frankfurt, 1985. Mock-up of a mid-range saloon car.

Alien, Turin 1986. Design for a sports car with transverse centrally-mounted engine starting at 1600 cc, length 369 cm.

IAD was founded back in 1968 but it took 10 years for them to open a styling unit. They made their first public appearance at the 1980 Birmingham Motor Show and nobody would have guessed by looking at the TRX, a banal design based on the TR7, just how much the company would expand. It went from two hundred employees in 1982 to more than 700 just five years later! IAD provides manufacturers with the usual design and engineering services, from preliminary styling designs, solid or hollow mock-ups, prototypes and the final tooling up. From their shaky beginnings the IAD team, under Eddie Pepall, have shown off their progress at successive Motor Shows. Their first projects were intended mainly to establish the technical credibility of the firm, so their early output consisted of wind tunnel models. Then in Frankfurt in 1985, IAD showed its expertise in computer-aided design when it proposed the "Arrival" aerodynamic saloon car designed entirely on screen. Today IAD has more than 30 workstations. After its first discreet foray in 1984 with the Volvo LCP 2000 design, the firm had no hesitation in showing up at the 1986 Turin Motor Show to niggle the Italian coachworks with a dream car called the Alien. This invader, designed by Martin Longmore and Marcus Hotback, was an interesting play of shapes, with the rear end visually separated from the passenger compartment by the use of different materials, colours and shape. Then in 1987, IAD offered the public two original designs for an all-terrain vehicle at the Frankfurt Motor Show. The most radical was the Impact with its contoured cockpit sitting on top of the mechanical structure (along

Impact, Frankfurt 1987. All-
terrain vehicle built on the
mechanical structure of the

Ford Sierra 4WD. V6 engine,
2.8 litres, 150 hp, four-wheel
drive, length 414 cm.

the lines of Giugiaro's Capsula), while the most restrained one was called the Interstate. The Impact project resurfaced in Turin in 1988 as a soft-top dubbed the Hunter. In contrast to these rather brutish devices, IAD is also capable of putting together an elegant and classical saloon, the Royale, based on the Subaru and built with the collaboration of Philips for the electronic equipment.

Many manufacturers have turned to IAD, including Audi, Matra, Rover, Porsche, Reliant, Saab, Volvo and Ford. Rolls-Royce was another customer; in 1985, Ken Greenley and John Hefferman dreamed up the Bentley P90 coupé which could have taken over the mantle of the Continental from the 1950s. For Panther the same stylists designed the Solo (1984).

Today, IAD can lay claim to being the foremost British design firm. In any event chairman John W. Shute certainly runs things in appropriate style from his headquarters in Worthing on the south coast.

Royale, Turin 1988. Luxury
saloon built on the
mechanical structure of the
Subaru Alcyone. Six
cylinder 2.7 litre engine.

Length 505 cm.
Sophisticated navigation
equipment, hi-fi and video
developed with the
cooperation of Philips.

**Rover is now associated with Honda and has everything to gain from a marriage which brings together technology and tradition, and puts the chaos of the past firmly behind it.**

Rover 800 series, sketch of the dashboard, September 1986. Computer-aided design.

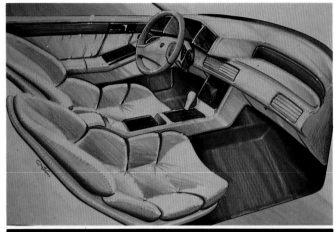

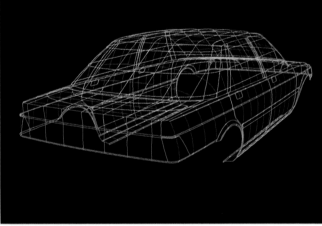

MG EX-E, Frankfurt 1985. Small saloon built on the mechanical structure of the MG Metro 6R4. Centrally-mounted V6 engine, 3 litres, 253 hp turbo, 24 valves.

Following double page: Rover CCV: Turin 1986. Design for a coupé based on the 800 series.

**B**y the time it came under the control of British Aerospace in the spring of 1988, Rover had been through troubled times. The history of the British car industry is a catalogue of mergers, take-overs and lost companies. In 1968, British Leyland Motors Corporation was born of the merger of Standard-Triumph, Rover, Jaguar-Daimler and BMC which itself was a combination of Austin, Morris, MG, Riley and Wolseley. One management team after another gradually reorganised things. After endless restructuring, the company which has become the Rover Group now comprises only MG and Rover; the other names have just disappeared, while Jaguar was given its freedom and took flight in 1984. Fragmented among all these separate names, British Leyland styling was running into the ground until it found a new lease of life in 1982, thanks to Royden Axe. A dyed-in-the-wool Englishman, born in Lincolnshire in 1937, he started his career with Rootes and patiently worked his way up the corporate ladder to become head of the design centre when Chrysler took over. Axe was in charge of all the European branches of Chrysler between 1970 and 1976, and was responsible for the design of several Simca models (1307 and the Horizon in particular) and the Sunbeams of the same period. In 1976 he vacated his place to Arthur Blakeslee and headed for Chrysler in the United States before returning to England to guide the destiny of what was then the Austin Rover Group, succeeding David Bache. Axe arrived in the Canley design department at the very time when Austin-Rover was negotiating a decisive and delicate manoeuvre. In November 1982, the British group signed an

agreement with Honda with the aim of undertaking a joint design programme, the "XX", which would lead to the production of two top-of-the-range cars sharing the same mechanical structure. It is true that the Triumph Acclaim and the Rover "200" series were already fruits of the same link-up, but these two saloons were little more than variations on the Honda Ballade, whereas the more ambitious "XX" programme provided

for the design of two complete and distinct styling designs to be produced in parallel in Japan and Great Britain. This process resulted in the Honda Accord and the Rover 800; the latter appeared in October 1986, a year after its Japanese cousin, with an undeniably British touch in the choice of materials for the passenger compartment. The Canley design centre had put Rover right back in the international pack. Before all this, Roy-

den Axe's team had lived up to its promise by unveiling a spectacular prototype at the 1984 Birmingham Motor Show: the MGE-XE small saloon based on the mechanical structure of the MG Metro GR4.

Austin Rover is back on the way to the regaining the name which it had lost in the vicissitudes of history.

**You must bear in mind that when the term ''Scandinavian Design'' is used, it refers to features of everyday living; cars are not one of them.**

Saab EV-1, Los Angeles 1985. Four-seater coupé built on the mechanical structure of the 900 Turbo 16. Length 430 cm, weight 1150 kg, Cx 0.32.

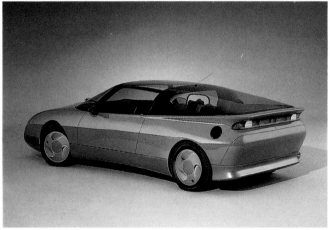

Saab Speeder 1986. Built by Mellberg Custom AB coachworks on the mechanical structure of the 900 Turbo 16S. (2 litres, 230 hp).

Scandinavian design earned its place by bringing craft into the art of living; it turned to natural materials with their rural connotations, humanising an environment which had been taken over by metal and plastic. The Swedish car industry no doubt benefitted from this mood but the actual reality of it needs a rather more detailed analysis.

The country's two manufacturers, Saab and Volvo, have barely anything in common other than a strong and original image. For Saab, their background in aircraft is crucial; the car sector was set up after the war and used aerodynamics as its spearhead. Sixten Sason designed every Saab up until he died and was succeeded by Björn Envall, a former art school student, in 1969. His studios are now set up in a wooden house which looks more like a woodcutter's cabin than a design centre. As novelties are something of a rarity at Saab, their stylists wanted to show their maturity with the EV-1 prototype unveiled in May 1985 in Los Angeles. What really distinguished this realistic and comfortable vehicle was an air conditioning system run by solar cells set into the roof. It was something of a consolation for the Saab Design Centre, which lost out to Giugiaro in the competition to design the 9000.

Volvo has built its name on two allied values coined by two key words: safe and solid. Designers put this message across by designing heavy, imposing cars. There are two separate teams shaping the future with two different sensibilities. In the Swedish town of Gothenburg, Jan Wilsgaard's stylists design the top-of-the-range models with an American flavour. In the Dutch town of Helmond, a team of seven stylists headed by Rob Koch designs smaller and more innovative models (480 ES, 440).

Volvo LCP 2000, 1983.
Design worked out in
collaboration with I.A.D..
Three-cylinder turbo
engine, 1.4 litres, 88 hp or
turbodiesel 1.3 litres, 52 hp.
Length 398 cm, Cx 0.28.
Total weight 645 kg,
including 178 kg of
aluminium, around 170 kg of
plastics and 43 kg of
magnesium.

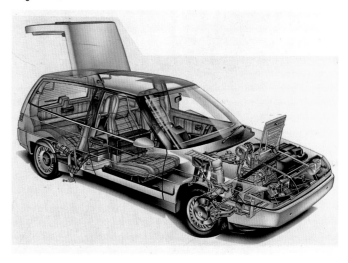

Even the advanced designs unveiled by Volvo are not exempt
from strict pragmatism. In 1976, Volvo took part in a taxi competition organised by the Museum of Modern Art in New York.
In late 1983, the LCP 2000 prototype produced jointly with the
British firm IAD (like the 440) brought the use of new materials
up to date; particular emphasis was placed on magnesium,
which can be obtained by the electrolysis of sea water.

But isn't this all rather lacking in imagination?

Saab EV-1. The mechanical      made of ultralight elastic
structure is the same as the   composite material (plastic
900 Turbo 16 (4 cylinders, 2   reinforced with aramid
litres, 285 hp). Headlamps     fibres).
designed by Hella, bumpers

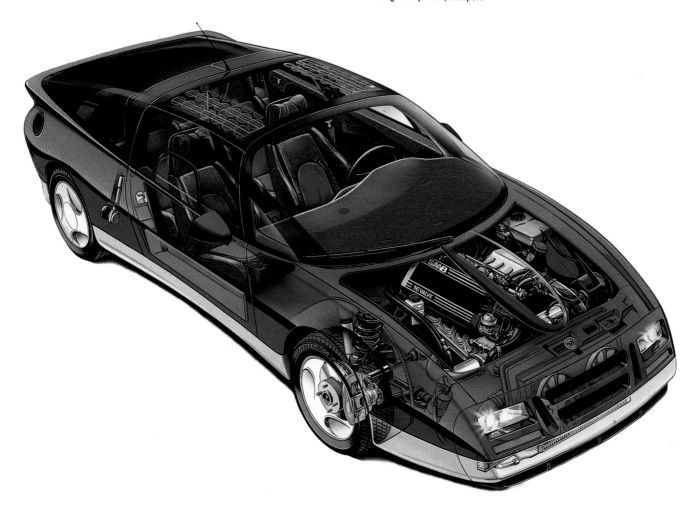

Without technology, design can only produce knick-knacks. But Germany is protected from such risks because its designers have a moral obligation to keep up the pioneering aerodynamic work of their predecessors.

**Porsche Design and the Porsche Styling Studio should not be confused. These two arms of Porsche apply their intelligence to serve all aspects of industrial creation.**

Below: Anatole Lapine, photographed at General Motors in the late 1950s when he was working on the Chevrolet Corvette "Shark" prototype.

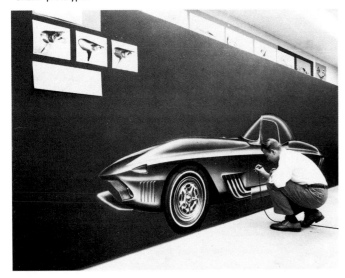

Porsche 911 Speedster, Frankfurt 1987. Pre-production prototype which went on the market in 1989.

Derived from the 911 Carrera, 6 cylinder rear engine, 3.2 litres, 231 hp, 245 kph.

Opposite: the same Tony Lapine in 1988 with the model for the Porsche 911 speedster.

Nobody at the Porsche Styling Studio in Weissach suffers from the "designer" complex. The men who design cars are proud to call themselves "stylists". This is far from being the case at Porsche Design, which is completely independent of the Porsche factory. It was created in 1972 by Ferdinand Alexander Porsche, 37 at the time, a graduate of the respectable school of Ulm and grandson of Ferdinand, the "Professor" who made the dynasty famous. At its chalet in Zell-am-See, high in the Austrian Alps, Porsche Design carries out two activities: designing and producing objects bearing the Porsche name and producing products for other firms. Watches, spectacles, pens, pipes, a NEC telephone, a camera for Yashica, lamps for Luci in Milan — an anthology of contemporary objects to which the Pompidou Centre in Paris devoted an exhibition in September 1987. Cars are not part of the brief of Porsche Design, even though Ferdinand Alexander Porsche ("Butzi") had run the styling studio from 1960 before coming to Porsche Design. He was behind the 904 Carrera GTS and in particular the immortal 911, which celebrated its 25th birthday in September 1988.

Other hands modelled it, burnished it, improved it and caricatured it. Anatole Lapine took over from Butzi Porsche

Below and opposite:
<u>Porsche 959</u>, Frankfurt 1983.
2+2 coupé with production
limited to 250. 6 cylinder
turbo engine, 2.85 litres, 450
hp, electronically-
controlled integrated
transmission. Speed 315
kph, Cx 0.31.

Porsche 911 Carrera, with
special features (935-type
bonnet) provided by
Porsche's "Sonderwünsch"
department.

in 1972. He was born in the Baltic port of Riga in 1930, but his family cleverly made a strategic move to Hamburg at the beginning of the war. He was working as a mechanic in Lincoln, Nebraska in 1951 and then decided to try his luck with the Styling Staff at General Motors. He had a hand in designing several very special Corvettes and one Sunday, Bill Mitchell even lent him the keys of a prototype Stingray so that he could ride the Elkhart Lake circuit. Despite all this special treatment, Tony Lapine decided to return to Europe in 1965, coming back on the same aircraft as Clare MacKirchan, a designer who had been involved in the Corvette '53 and had just been appointed to Opel. Lapine joined Porsche styling in 1969 and rose to head it when Butzi Porsche went off on his Austrian adventure. That same year, 1972, the research unit left the confines of Zuffenhausen and moved to Weissach, also in the Stuttgart area. Helmut Bott is director of this enormous pool of ideas, which works for the whole world in fields as varied as military equipment, aviation and fire engines. The outfit operates in an ultramodern building formed of three hexagons. Tony Lapine is assisted by Peter Reisinger, chief model-maker and Wolfgang Möbius, who is in charge of exterior styling. This team sculpted the voluptuous 928, then went on to play variations on the 911 theme. The 930 Turbo (1977), the 959 (1983), the 911 Carrera Speedster (1987) and the Carrera 4 (1988) are high-powered cadenzas on that theme.

**Mercedes cars, produced by the sober Daimler-Benz company, pay perpetual respect to the Three-pointed Star.**

Mercedez-Benz W124, November 1984. Computer-assisted design for saloon in W124 range, which includes the 200 and 300 models.

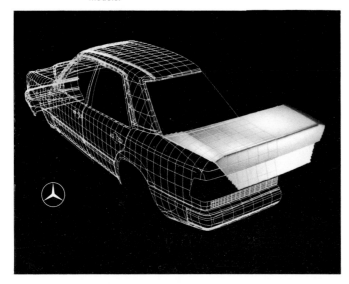

Mercedes-Benz Forschungswagen, Frankfurt 1981. Prototype of an aerodynamic hatchback saloon based on the 500 SE. Engines either V6 3.8 litre 149 hp turbodiesel or turbine. Length 510 cm, Cx 0.30.

At the time when the "190" was launched in January 1983, Bruno Sacco was preparing to celebrate his first quarter century with Daimler-Benz in Sindelfingen. His severe face, fringed with a close, grey beard, tends to light up suddenly; he cannot betray his Italian origins. He was born in Udine in 1933 but took German nationality in 1975. He studied engineering at the *Politecnico* in Turin and took his first steps as a stylist with Moretti and Ghia coachworks. In 1957, Sacco met Karl Wilfert, head of the "body design" department at Daimler-Benz and shyly asked him if there was any chance of getting a bit of experience; Wilfert said yes and Sacco has never left Sindelfingen since then. Mercedes styling now has two branches, form and technology, which employ around 60 stylists and model-makers and about 25 technicians respectively. The "190" marked the arrival of Mercedes in a new market and used all the subtle techniques of design to reconcile opposites: lightness and sturdiness, modernity and tradition, conformism and aerodynamics. The W124 range, which covers the 200 and 300 models, was even more refined than the 190, with a Cx reduced from 0.33 to 0.29. This is the way each generation progresses, both invisible and radical at the same time, without calling in outside consultants. This proud attitude expresses all the confidence of a company which believes in its lucky star.

# B M W

**Being obsessed with a brand image inevitably blocks progress. BMW, like Mercedes, feels that it has to clothe high technology in sober garments.**

The unchanging double radiator grille has been the rallying point for all BMWs since the beginning of the 1930s. This fixed smile is more than just a mannerism; it actually expresses the burden of conservatism. Just like their rivals from Stuttgart, the development of BMW cars proceeds at a measured pace; in the aftermath of the energy crisis, BMW was definitely lagging behind its rivals on the aerodynamic front. In their world crammed with technology, the engineers quickly regained the upper hand. In 1981 BMW established a new aerothermic centre and the 7 and 5 series saloons, launched in 1986 and 1988, scored very respectable drag coefficient figures. Since the departure of Paul Bracq, Claus Luthe has been the obedient keeper of the BMW image although during the years when the 5 and 7 series were on the drawing board, the Italian stylist Ercole Spada was the standard bearer before he left to join I.DE.A. In a move to break with convention, BMW created an autonomous department, BMW Technik GmbH, and gave it a free hand. The team came up with the ZI, a spartan sports car which revived the spirit of 1950s sports cars which emphasised pleasure at the expense of comfort. The ZI is built on a steel monocoque structure on which a plastic floor was bonded, with a moulded composite body.

The fact that BMW management encouraged the marketing of the ZI was an admission that the car industry needed a breath of fresh air.

BMW ZI, June 1986. Prototype of a sports car designed by BMW Téchnik GmbH and marketed from 1989. Front-mounted 6 cylinder engine, 2.5 litres, 170 hp. Length 392 cm, speed 230 kph.

Mock-up of an aerodynamic small saloon car built to mark the inauguration of the new BMW aerothermic centre (AVT) in 1981.

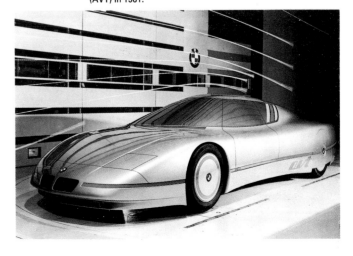

The German Creators

**Audi and Volkswagen are part of the same group, V.A.G., but family feeling is no guarantee against sibling rivalry.**

Audi Forschungswagen, Frankfurt 1981. Prototype for an aerodynamic saloon car preceeding the Audi 100 launched at the 1982 Paris

Car Show. Aerodynamic body (Cx 0.30) with flush side windows. Front-wheel drive, engine 1.6 turbo 110 hp, length 476 cm.

Volkswagen Auto 2000, Frankfurt 1981. Prototype for an economy vehicle built in accordance with directives from the BMFT. Front-wheel drive, three-

cylinder diesel 1191 cc engine, 45 hp, or four-cylinder turbo injected 1050 cc 75 hp. Speed 150-180 kph. Length 401 cm.

There is no geographical proximity between the two marques; VW is located in the Hanover area near the East-West border, while Audi is set in the heart of Bavaria in Ingolstadt. Since the merger in 1974 there has been a tradition of fierce competition stimulating the rival cousins. Outside broad policy lines, each of the two branches of V.A.G. leads its own life with its own engineers (Fiala at VW and Piëch at Audi) and its own stylists. At the turn of the decade, Audi and Volkswagen were forced to turn their aim against a common enemy – fuel consumption – with the Federal Ministry for Research and Technology spurring German manufacturers to work on fuel economy. This yielded tangible results at the 1981 Frankfurt Motor Show in the shape of the Audi Forschungswagen, fore-runner of the Audi 100 (1982) and a Volkswagen Auto 2000 heralding the Golf II (1983). Since 1972, VW-Design has been run by Herbert Schäffer, a technician who came to Wolfsburg in 1960 to lead a quiet career as a administrator looking after relations with outside consultants. After the period of uprisings during which Giorgetto Giugiaro invented the first Golf (1974), Volkswagen was purring along again. Every now and then VW would lift the wraps on one of its advanced designs. The 1984 version was called the Student and the 1986 version the Scooter. In late 1985 the French designer Patrick Le Quément had a spell at VW to set up a research unit in Düsseldorf. A more concrete development came in 1986 when VW set up a new wind tunnel fitted with robots and lasers and intended for aerothermic studies. The Orbit model was the first project to come from this new wind tunnel. Aerodynamics has become the password at VW and the Passat launched in 1988 has done its job properly with a Cx of 0.29.

The top man at Audi is Helmut Warkuss. For Audi, styling is given a higher priority than at VW and refinement is more important than functionalism. Consequently, aerodynamic work is more subtle. The Audi 100, for example, earned its

place in the record books with a Cx of 0.30 but its silhouette was still classical; the only visible innovation was the flush-mounted windows. The Audi 80 presented in 1986 is the antithesis of the VW Passat; capacity has been sacrificed but no effort has been spared with styling. Audi deserves a special mention for its fight against body rust; all panels are galvanised, which involves them being covered with a fine layer of zinc. The art of coach-building sometimes goes well beyond the drawing board.

**Volkswagen Student,** Geneva 1984. Prototype urban economy car. The number of separate elements forming the body has been kept to a minimum. Engine four cylinders, 1100 cc, 50 or 75 hp, length 313 cm, speed 157 to 178 kph. Cx 0.30.

**Volkswagen Orbit,** 1988. Wind tunnel model put together in the new Volkswagen aerothermic centre: Cx 0.16.

**Volkswagen Scooter,** Geneva 1986. Fun car. Transverse front-mounted engine, 4 cylinders, 1050 cc or 1400 cc. Length 317 cm, 550 kg, Cx 0.25.

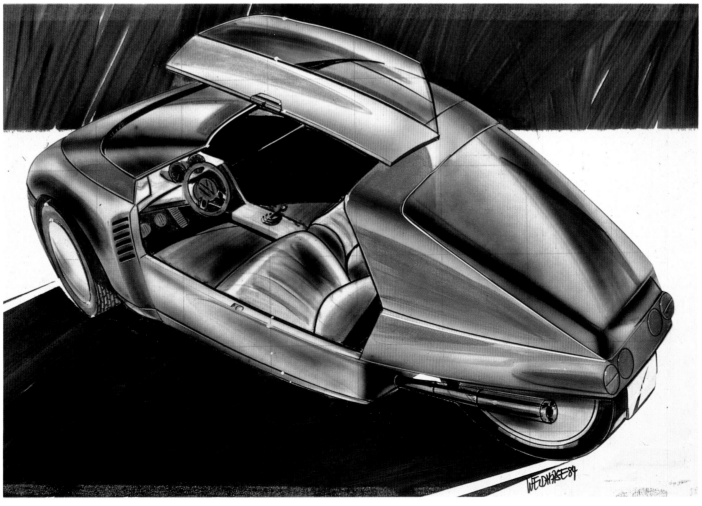

George Gallion, in charge of the Adam Opel Design Center headed in succession by Henry Higgs, Gordon Brown and Wayne Cherry.

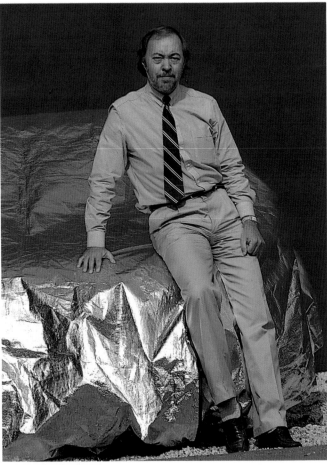

Tech 1, Frankfurt 1981. Aerodynamic four-seater saloon based on the mechanical structure of the Opel Kadett, length 431 cm, Cx 0.24.

**Opel acts as a listening post for General Motors in Europe. They suddenly realised that design was a condition of future strength.**

Adam Opel Design Center occupies a geometrical building situated in the heart of the immense factory complex in Rüsselsheim and painted in the company colours, light grey and yellow. Opel Design owes its allegiance to the GM Design Centre Detroit, so the men who follow one another into the director's office are mostly sent from the United States. The young American designer Gordon Brown was called to Rüsselsheim in July 1980 to take over from his compatriot Henry Haga, who went off to California to look after advanced styling. Brown went missing in a mountain accident in May 1983 at the age of 42. Wayne Cherry left the English unit, Vauxhall, to guide the destiny of Opel. One constant in these three changes has been the presence of the number two, George Gallion, who trained at the Georgia Institute of Technology. The Design Center employs roughly two hundred people including about thirty designers from 10 different counties, the idea being to be familiar with all the different types of taste, worldwide. There are four studios, with the first looking after the small Corsa and Kadett models, the second dealing with the middle category (Ascona, Manta, Vectra) and the third in charge of top-of-the-range models (Omega and Senator). The fourth studio looks to the future with advanced styling and competition.

Opel is one of the marques which used design as a powerful tool to relaunch itself. In the space of a few years, Opel cars have made considerable progress on the technical front which has been echoed in the streamlined shapes of the cars. The Kadett (0.30) and the Omega (0.28) could prove rather disconcerting for customers who are used to something rather more old-fashioned. This courageous commercial policy was announced ahead of several prototypes. The Kadett which came out in 1984 owed much to the Tech 1, which was shown at the 1981 Frankfurt Motor Show. The Junior did not go any further commercially but showed that Opel was looking into minimal cars for young people.

Above: <u>Tech 1</u>. Below and following double page: <u>Junior</u>, Frankfurt 1983. Based on a shortened Corsa platform; engine 1200 cc, 55 hp, length 341 cm, Cx 0.31. The dashboard is fitted to take cube-shaped plug-in modules (clock, rev counter etc).

Both in Europe and in the United States, General Motors is putting its money on innovative design and the enthusiastic reception from the customers shows that all the faint hearts in marketing were wrong.

**It always comes down to the basic alternatives which designers face: innovation or continuity. Ford has made its choice.**

Escort, October 1980. Sketch of the mass-production car for the world market. Engines 1100 to 1600, length 397 cm. Cx 0.375 for the XR3 version.

Probe III, Frankfurt 1981. Aerodynamic prototype for the Sierra. Length 464 cm, Cx 0.22.

ord bears an old grudge against General Motors which dates from the time when GM snatched the number one spot some time back, since when the number two car maker has been battling to catch up. Ford chose to make the best of the energy crisis by carrying out a stage-by-stage revolution both in Europe and in the United States. First there was the lure of the "World Car" which took the form of the Escort, launched on both sides of the Atlantic in October 1980. General Motors, Chrysler and Renault had the same ambition, but unlike them, Ford managed to market the same product with a very distinctive appearance. In 1982, they made another change of tack which flew in the face of conventional marketing wisdom; they replaced the very conventional Taunus and Cortina with an original and highly aerodynamic design, the Sierra. The company had started down this path in 1979 with the "Probe" series of prototypes and the Probe III, shown at the 1981 Frankfurt Motor Show, was the direct predecessor of the Sierra. The prime mover behind this courageous policy was Uwe Bahnsen, who was backed up by Robert Lutz, chairman of Ford Europe (who later left to become Lee Iacocca's right-hand-man at Chrysler). Bahnsen was born in Hamburg in 1930 and studied at the school of Fine Art before joining Ford in 1958. His stentorian voice, just right for country music, called the tune for Ford-Europe stylists between 1976 and 1986 before moving on to start a new career at the Art Center in Vevey. There are two studios for Ford-Europe design; exterior styling is carried out at Merkenich near Cologne, while interior styling and industrial vehicles remain the prerogative of Dunton in Great Britain. Apart from its two European centres and Ghia in Italy, Ford also has studios in Australia and Brazil.

Eltec, Frankfurt 1985. Investigation into the use of electronic technology. Four-cylinder 12-valve engine, 1.3 litres, 80 hp, length 412 cm, Cx 0.31.

From 1981 Bahnsen was backed up in Merkenich by a French designer, Patrick Le Quément, who was born in 1945 and graduated in industrial design from Birmingham Polytechnic. He spent two years training at Simca before joining Ford of Europe in 1968. Le Quément was deeply involved in the design of the controversial and daring Scorpio, then he left Ford. When Bahnsen left, Andrew K. Jacobson moved into the office of vice-president of design, but his work belongs to the 1990s.

Preliminary sketch for the Scorpio, launched in March 1985. Engines from 2.0 litres to 2.8 litres, length 467 cm, Cx 0.33.

149

**Eberhard Schulz doesn't design cars to be filed away in albums. He wants to see his cars living, moving and proliferating. That's why he created Isdera.**

Imperator 108i, Geneva 1984. Limited production small saloon, centrally-mounted Mercedes-Benz 5-litre V8 engine, later 5.6 litres. Approximately 280 kph, length 422 cm, Cx 0.38.

Eberhard Schulz holding up the tubular chassis of the Imperator 108i.

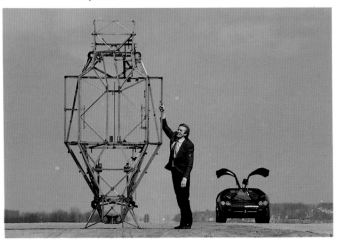

W armbronn is a peaceful little town near Stuttgart, hidden in the forests of Baden-Würtemberg, with a romantic feeling lent by nearby Solitude castle. However, more practical considerations brought Eberhard Schulz to the Loenberg area. It is midway between Zuffenhausen and Sindelfingen, which means equidistant from Porsche and Mercedes-Benz, not to mention Bosch, Recaro and other big names in the car industry which have also settled in the area.

In 1981, Eberhard Schulz had just turned 40 when he founded Ingenieurbüro für Styling, Design und Racing, or Isdera. Schulz's career has tended more towards technology than fine arts. His engineering training gained him an entrée at Porsche, where he was taken on by the styling centre as a "studio engineer". His dual capabilities of engineer/designer were put to work in May 1968 to build a coupé dubbed the Erator GTE, with a polyester body over a tubular chassis of his own design and a Beetle engine. Schulz then developed a competition side-car in collaboration with the University of Stuttgart. Painstaking work in the wind tunnel brought the Cx down to 0.234; Schulz has always taken a lot of care to make his creations aerodynamic. Being attracted by competition, he submitted several designs to AMG, who specialise in Mercedes-Benz, and set up the 450 SL for group 2 to race the 1978 season.

An important break in Schulz's career came when he shook hands with Rainer and Dieter Buchmann. These two businessmen dreamed of seeing their name on the side of a car but they needed Schulz to do it, because the two brothers did not have a spark of creativity between them. The young designer dreamed up a sort of reincarnated Mercedes-Benz 300 SL, then traced out the plans, built the mock-up and assembled the chassis. All the Buchmann brothers had to do was fix their double "B" at the four corners of the car, which was dubbed the CW 311 and was powered by a Mercedes-Benz 6.3 litre engine developing 375 hp. The Schulz-Buchmann association lasted for three years until the spring of 1981, by which time 'BB' had an enviable reputation. He put together a track motorbike for Kreidler and for Sauber he designed the C6, a closed car for endurance racing in the 1982 season. For Pirelli he designed a wheel rim on which the cooling ducts formed a stylised "P"; this became a popular feature on the Golf GTI. He then went on to design accessories sold by Porsche's "special orders" department.

By the time he founded Isdera, Eberhard Schultz therefore had three trump cards: technical expertise, a love of racing and a gift for styling. He laid the three cards on the table and made his bid: to become a "manufacturer". The first Isdera was the Spyder 033i, which appeared at the 1983 Geneva Motor Show; its lines were like an off-shore speedboat. One year later, the CW311 prototype reappeared under a different name, the Imperator 108i, for limited series production and marketing. Henceforth, Isdera productions distinguished themselves by the neatness of their mechanical finish; neatness and simplicity are the features of their construction, based on a square-section tubular framework.

Schulz loves competition and it shows. He is very proud of the special relationship he has with Daimler-Benz and this is not surprising when you realise how much mistrust there is in Stuttgart for anybody who plays around with the three-pointed star of Mercedes-Benz. Schulz was allowed to use the Mercedes wind tunnel to perfect the bodywork of the Imperator. Without using any tricks, without a spoiler and with a huge air intake, the Imperator scored a Cx figure of 0.381. All Isderas are powered by Mercedes-Benz engines; in the Spyder 033-16 it's the 2.3-16 engine from the 190E, the Spyder 036i has the 6-cylinder unit from the 300 E. As for the Imperator, it is powered by the V8 from the 560 SEC, while the Commendator for the 1990s will boast a V12!

Following double page:
Imperator 108i.
Below: the first sketches for the small saloon powered by the Mercedes-Benz 12-cylinder unit.

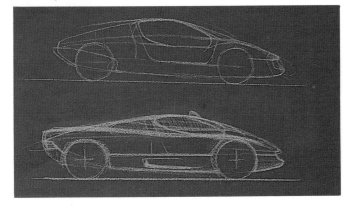

Putting together the mock-up of the Commendator 112 in the Spring of 1988.

The BMW TC-3 in the
Daimler-Benz wind tunnel
in February 1987 (Cx 0.298).

Above, below and opposite:
BMW TC-3 designed by
Isdera for Baur. 6-cylinder

2.5 litre 170 hp engine,
bodywork made of Kevlar.

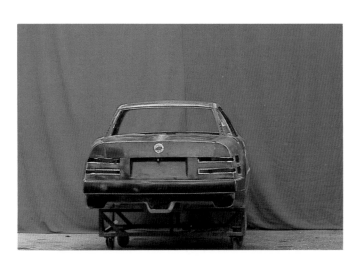

A rather unusual story began in 1983 when Baur coachworks, who had worked with BMW for many years, launched the "TC3" programme. Baur is a firm with a reputation for building special bodies but it has never felt any particular urge to be creative, so when they wanted to pin down the idea of the BMW TC3, they turned to Isdera. The car hit the road for the first time in February 1987. The BMW TC3 is a coupé with disconcerting, personal lines emphasised by some very special motifs. The system of sticking on the windows allows for some interesting variations in style, and the aerodynamics are of course carefully worked out. The results obtained with the BMW TC3 in the Daimler-Benz wind tunnel are encouraging: a Cx of 0.298 and a S.Cx of 0.533. The body is made of Kevlar while the mechanical elements are taken from the BMW 325i. The mass-produced parts are grafted onto a tubular frame made of rigid steel inspired by the Isdera design.

When the BMW TC3 was finished in February 1987, BMW had announced its ZI roadster six months beforehand. The TC3 project was dropped but the design surfaced again bearing the Irmscher mark at the 1988 Geneva Motor Show.

In September 1987 Eberhard established a foothold in Long Island, Isdera of North America Inc., which should create some new openings for the young company. Isdera is doing nicely, there is no shortage of projects and a good mood prevails in the workshops. Frau Schulz takes care of the secretarial side while Eberhard is to be found amidst his dozen or so employees lending a hand to the production of Isdera cars (the seventeenth Imperator and eleventh Spyder in mid-1988). In a corner of the workshop, two adolescent model-makers are putting together a competition sidecar made of polyester. They are Olaf and Ulf, Eberhard's children. In this country where design still takes a back seat to technology, Schulz has a wise approach; he tries his hand in a discreet and courteous way, with his children playing by his side.

# ZENDER

**In the hazy world of German coachworks, Zender stands out from the opportunists.**

In 1969, Hans Albert Zender set up a small firm specialising in designing, producing and distributing accessories (skirts, dams and other aerodynamic items). This was a lucrative, rather unexciting business and Zender might well have been satisfied with it since the birth of the Golf GTI created an avalanche of demand for his products. However, in 1978 Zender decided to engage the services of a *real* designer, Günther Zillner, who had served his apprenticeship with Ford and designed several competition cars (Ford C100, Kauhsen F1 etc.). This immediately gave Zender products added cachet, and proper styling backed up by wind tunnel testing enabled Zender to stand out from the mass of accessory manufacturers. In 1983, the Zender-Zillner duo took the plunge by designing a wholly original new body to fit the Audi Quattro base. The Vision 1 was unveiled at the 1983 Frankfurt Motor Show. Two years later, they showed the mock-up of a much more ambitious small saloon built round a centrally-mounted engine. The Vision 2 was then slightly modified to become the Vision 3 in 1986 and the open-top 3C. The following year, a Mercedes-Benz engine was finally added to the mock-up. The lines of the car were still angular and aggressive, but also personal. And there is no doubt that they were the lines of a creator, not an accessory manufacturer.

Zender Vision 3, Frankfurt 1987. Two-seater saloon with centrally-mounted Mercedes-Benz V8 5.6 litre engine, 300 hp. Cx of 0.342, recorded in the Daimler-Benz wind tunnel.

Preceding double page:
<u>Koenig GT-Competition</u>,
Geneva 1988. Berlinetta
developed from the Ferrari
Testarossa. 12-cylinder
turbo engine, 800 hp. Below
<u>Ferrari Testarossa and
Porsche 911 "Cyrrus"</u> as
transformed by Gemballa.

<u>Treser Roadster</u>, Frankfurt
1985. Sports car with fold-
away hardtop, produced in
small numbers. Centrally-

mounted engine taken from
the Golf GTI 16V 1.8 litre,
130 hp. 210 kph, length 404
cm.

**Germany is the home of technology and quality, but they appear to regard the coachbuilder's art as something foreign. The few craftsmen working in this field go for frivolous effects.**

Germany has never been the first choice for coach-builders. Admittedly, before the war there were exceptions like Erdmann & Rossi and a few others, but as a rule innovation was never a characteristic of coachbuilders but rather the product of the laboratories of great aerodynamicists such as Wunibald Kamm or Paul Jaray. The same split between scientists and coachbuilders persists to this day. Rather than staking out the high ground of creativity, German coachbuilders often prefer to take the easy option of "tuning" (involving mechanical and aesthetic alterations made to personalise mass-produced cars). The process was triggered off by the appearance of the Golf GTI in 1974. With this functional small saloon car, sports cars acquired a new status with the abandonment of the special look which GT coupés used to have.

The GTI was delivered with a rather perfunctory set of equipment (round headlights, plain rims); it was therefore an ideal candidate for "tuning" and many accessories manufacturers seized their opportunity with both hands. Soon all German sports cars were being given the same treatment. To the delight of some of the oil-producing countries, the fashion spread to even richer parts and Mercedes and Porsche were given the treatment. An excess of luxury left the field wide open to vulgarity, bad taste and excesses of every description. All

Porsche 928 S4,
transformed by Vittorio
Strosek (in the photo) in
1988.

sorts of little outfits opened up to dispense various custom features and scarlet leather to even the most dignified of limousines. Then the bubble burst and the trend came to an end, but it left ugly traces; saloon cars started to sprout all sorts of appendages.

Tuning was soon turning its attentions to even the most established myths. Firms like Gemballa and Koenig showed a certain talent in their transfiguration of the sacrosanct Ferrari Testarossa; the lines of the car were purified by the former and given a more aggressive look by the latter. Some people regarded this as treason, but certain transformations are able to mould the personality of the original work and sublimate it.

Apart from these master jesters, there are few independent designers in Germany. Walter Treser made his bid to escape from the tuning ghetto by designing an unusual roadster in 1987; Friedrich Peter Lorenz chose another way out in 1985 when he created the Silver Falcon, a convertible with a touch of the Fifties about it marketed as a "Lorenz & Rankl" machine.

The big industrial design companies like Delta Design, Target Design, Frog Design and Hans Muth virtually ignore cars. In Germany as elsewhere, cars are an ambiguous product.

Lorenz & Rankl Silver
Falcon, Frankfurt 1985.
Limited production
convertible. Kevlar and
aluminium body, tubular
chassis, front-mounted
Mercedes-Benz V8 5 litre
engine, 240 hp, wheelbase
240 cm. Upholstery of
ostrich skin. Following
double page: Ferrari
Testarossa by Gemballa,
Geneva 1988.

**Is Luigi Colani a genius or an imposter? There can be only one answer once you accept that this megalomaniac is the most influential creative mind of his era.**

The forms of nature inspire all Luigi Colani's work, as shown by this X114 hydrofoil from 1973.

A streamlined motorcycle.

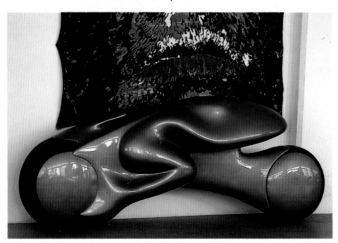

He's always talking about subversion but his approach is romantic, his life is a history of paranoia but his work is utopian. Luigi Colani cannot be fitted into the existing order of things. He cannot be compared with other designers, especially not for cars. Colani is somewhere else, on the borders, probably in the future. His greatness is not a tangible thing because he makes his point in the unconscious of his contemporaries. There is no inventory of his industrial creations because they are virtually non-existent. Colani's influence is hazy, more philosophical than anything else; he brings monuments crashing down, calls Pierre Cardin a "duty free shop designer" and Raymond Loewy the "prince charming of American ugliness".

Is Luigi Colani's soul unblemished enough to allow him to indulge in such invective? From his consistency, it would appear so; Colani has never gone back on his commitments, he has never made compromises with passing fashion. His conduct is straightforward, his work is logical and his curriculum vitae reads like a heretic's crusade. Luigi Colani was born in Berlin on 2 August 1928. From his father, a decorator, he inherited the family name from Ticino in Switzerland while his Polish mother endowed him with a slavic sensibility. Together they nurtured a taste for show and throughout his life, Colani has played the *role* of Colani. He studied painting and sculpture at the Berlin school of Fine Art then staged his first period of exile in France, which he says is a country of wit; there he developed his taste for provocation and contradiction. While working on illustrations for the magazine *Automobile*, he came into contact with Charles Deutsch and the university and discovered aerodynamics. Colani spent ten years in France, during which time he lived on a diet of culture and high technology. Around 1953 he returned to Germany to work at Rometsch and Erdmann & Rossi coachworks; he very soon threw himself into the production of the Colani GT Spyder model, the forerunner of a whole series of prototypes built on various mechanical structures during the 1950s.

In 1970 Luigi Colani set himself up in Harkotten castle in Füchtorf in surroundings worthy of him. It would be all too easy to define this noisy creator as just another eccentric. Colani sounds off against the pretentions of men, pours scorn on the vulgarity of design, thunders against the cowardice of industrialists and then suddenly prostrates himself before Nature: "Nature creates perfect designs", he proclaims, never deviating from this statement. "There are no straight lines in nature" is the creed of bio-design, which works with a vocabulary inspired by organic shapes with all their violence and sensuality.

Luigi Colani photographed
in May 1988.

The offices of Colani Design
Bern, in Switzerland.

When he outlines the basis of bio-design, Colani claims that he is doing nothing more than unearthing the range of forms suggested by Nature; he regards himself as a "humble" archaeologist of design. And perhaps also as the prophet of the great aesthetic faith of our time. When Colani talked about aerodynamics during the 1970s, nobody listened to him; people smiled at his "2001" style truck shown at the 1977 Frankfurt Motor Show. Now all truck manufacturers are doing their utmost to limit the wind resistance of their vehicles. In the

days when fashionable designers were drawing angular lines, Colani was regarded as an obsessive dreamer with his womb-like forms. In his world, everything is rounded: his aircraft, his motorbikes, his trains, his pens and his bathroom, marketed by Villeroy & Bosch.

In November 1967 he registered a patent for the C-Form, which consisted of a sort of folded wing enclosed in pontoons. Colani had sketched out the "wing car" which became commonplace in Formula 1 ten years later. From 1981 onwards, the C-Form was adapted to a number of different sports projects (GT 90, BMW M2, Colambo, Assym). One of these progressed beyond the model stage, a small saloon built on the mechanical structure of a Citroën 2CV; it reached a Cx of 0.17!

A number of firms have consulted Colani (Volkswagen, Audi, BMW) and he submitted radical proposals which nobody dared to put on the market – the same old story of top brass with cold feet. So Colani grew tired of the small-mindedness of his country and left everything behind: his castle and his country. In 1981 he went off to spread the word on the other side of the world and the Japanese welcomed him like a prophet. Every year in Matsumoto he addressed honourable ranks of dumbfounded designers, urging them to stop copying Europe and to delve into their past to rediscover the essentials of South Asia art. At conferences and gatherings of the faithful, Colani expounded the philosophy which was to become the "soft-line" which can now be seen everywhere in Japanese life. Working through his representative in Tokyo, the ODS company (Overseas Design Service), Luigi Colani has flooded every sector of industry: hi-fi (with Sony), photography (Canon), two-wheelers (Yamaha), golf (Daiwa), luggage (Skyway), glasses (Sunreeve), lighters (Yoshinaga), toys (Takara), telephones (NEC), bedding (Nishikawa Sangyo) etc. In the space of a few years, he became the most sought-after designer in Japan, leaving Giorgetto Giugiaro and Mario Bellini behind.

Finally he decided to return to the West so that he would no longer feel responsible for driving Europe to the wall, and also to continue his struggle against American imperialism, which is his hobbyhorse.

Previous double page: the Porsche 959 as seen by Luigi Colani in 1987.

Below: Mock-up built in 1986 for a small saloon with a centrally-mounted engine; aerodynamic body using ground effect. (C-Form). Development of the "Colambo" project.

Colani denounces the cultural influence of the United States. He will go to any lengths to block it: working for the Russians, teaching design in Peking, offering his services to Iran or Libya. Nobody could match the force with which Colani expresses his hatred and says who he dislikes. He is an iconoclast who uses design as a political weapon.

## A visionary of wide-open spaces

In the spring of 1987, Colani Design Bern moved to a workshop covering 2,500 square metres. The whole place was painted white, as if it were a screen on which he could project his arguments. He then proposed his version of the Porsche 959.

Dressed in white like an operetta sailor, with his Havana jutting before him like a figurehead, Colani moves around this scene of meticulous disorder. His models gather dust as they wait for a forthcoming exhibition. Dozens of publications litter the floor, each opened at the page where the Master is celebrated. A rag-bag of diverse objects are strewn around: here a baroque candelabra, there an ample sculpture. In an adjoining room, workers are finishing off a polyester model. But Bern already belongs to the past; the next stage will take Colani to Languedoc in the South of France in 1989. A return to France to send out more messages in bottles.

What is Colani doing in this world in this century? His only points of reference, Erté, Gaudi or Heironymus Bosch, have become timeless. The world of cars is no doubt too narrow for this visionary of open spaces. If Luigi Colani is not the greatest designer of this century and on earth, then maybe he ranks somewhere out there in the cosmos.

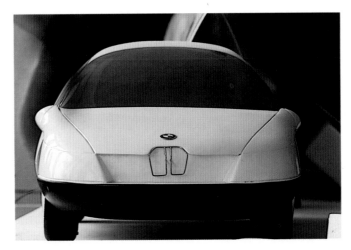

Proposed design for a
BMW 7 series.

Model of a vessel of the
future: half-bird, half-fish.

Toyota FX-1, Tokyo 1983. Small front engine saloon, 6 cylinders, 2 litres turbo, 24 valves 250 hp, separate chassis, Cx 0.25, hydropneumatic suspension with facility for altering ride height electronically to suit speed.

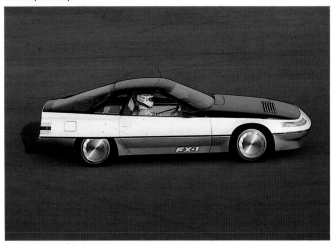

Having been fascinated by America and then inspired by Europe, Japanese design has begun to thrive by drawing on the roots of its own culture. Nowadays, Europe is condemned to copy Japan if it wants to avoid losing the economic war.

Toyota FXV, Tokyo 1985. Four-door saloon with centrally-mounted engine, 4 cylinders, 16 valves, turbocompressor linked to a mechanical compressor, 2 litres, 235 hp, integrated transmission. Length 478 cm. Cx 0.24.

Toyota FXV-II, Frankfurt 1987. Front-engine coupé, V8 3.8 litres, 32 valves, 235 hp, pneumatic suspension dropping by 2 cm at high speed, four-wheel drive, four-wheel steering, length 509 cm, Cx 0.26. The glasswork has an electrically conductive ceramic layer for demisting.

Westerners find it hard to accept a patchwork of East and West. However, the seven years of American occupation gave Japan a unique experience, provoking a change of behaviour even more radical than the one unleashed in 1868 by the Meiji restoration. The advent of prosperity was the starting point for Japan to change its life style and assimilate cultural influence imported in bulk. Nevertheless it took quite a long time for cars, a key element of the consumer society, to become a feature of Japanese customs. Initially it was the American look which tempted, then as the industrial dynamo began to turn in earnest in the Sixties, the Japanese turned to consult a number of Italian stylists: Giovanni Michelotti worked for Prince and Hino, Vignale counted Daihatsu among his clients, Giorgetto Giugiaro worked with Mazda under the Bertone banner then with Isuzu on behalf of Ghia; Pininfarina gave Nissan a hand, Tjaarda helped Isuzu and Sessano helped Mitsubishi. The Mediterranean breeze blowing through the styling departments swept away the American influence. The Japanese then sent their designers to study abroad, then they set up design studios in California: Toyota in Newport Beach in 1973, Honda in Torrance in 1974, Mazda in Irvine in 1976, Nissan in San Diego in 1979, Mitsubishi in Cypress and Isuzu in Cerritos in 1984 and finally Subaru in Garden Grove. As the end of the 1980s draws near, the Japanese have a production capacity of

To talk of Japanese style these days is to miss the point. Japan, which Roland Barthes called the empire of symbols, is initiating us into the mysteries of world-wide styling.

Above and following double page: <u>Isuzu COA-III,</u> Tokyo 1987. All-terrain sports car advocating "coexistence between nature and civilisation". Four cylinder 16 valve ceramic engine, 300 hp, four-wheel drive.

<u>Suzuki RT-1,</u> Tokyo 1987. Runabout sports car, 4-cylinder 1600 cc centrally-mounted engine, 16 valves, four-wheel drive, length 370 cm.

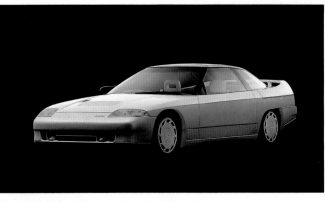

Mazda MX-03, Frankfurt 1985. 2+2 coupé with front rotary engine, turbo, three rotors, 3 × 654 cc, 320 hp, four-wheel drive, four-wheel steering, length 451 cm, Cx 0.25.

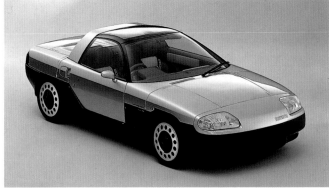

Mazda MX-04, Tokyo 1987. Modular car, developing from a sports car to a coupé. Two-rotor engine, 2 × 491 cc, length 383 cc.

Mitsubishi HSR, Tokyo 1987. Small saloon, 4 cylinders, 2 litres, 295 hp, four-wheel drive, four-wheel steering, length 460 cm, body made of Kevlar. Cx 0.20.

more than 1,600,000 vehicles on United States territory. Honda has been established in Ohio since 1982, Nissan in Tennessee since 1983, Toyota in California since 1984 and the Mazda factory has been operating in Flat Rock, Michigan since 1987. These examples show how Japan has turned to its own advantage the protectionist measures taken by the Reagan administration in 1981.

Even though the creativity of the Japanese occasionally seems to get caught up in repetition, they can still impress with their industrial power, their capacity to assimilate and even to anticipate trends, their ability to meet demands from all quarters, to industrialise at the drop of a hat and the ease with which they can beef up their styling designs with solid technological back-up. Throughout this decade, they have been busily acquiring advanced technology in every sphere: engines, electronics, materials, aerodynamics, etc. On the design front they

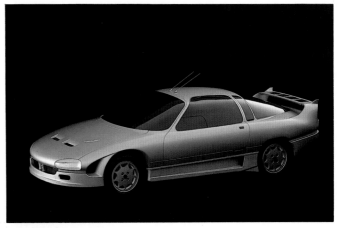

Subaru F-9X, Tokyo, 1985.
Small saloon with flat six
engine, four-wheel drive.

have pursued their investigations in every direction. Leisure cars, town cars and tourers, one-piece and modular designs, fun cars and utility vehicles are all examined. From a styling point of view, the dominant feature is without question a gradual move towards bio-design; Luigi Colani's stay in Tokyo has left indelible traces in the daily life of the Japanese. Their flexible production methods enable them to change body designs as often as every four years or so, and this inevitably has repercussions on public taste and on their capacity for innovation. The development in cars is proceeding hand in hand with a general transformation in aesthetics. These days the streets of Japan are echoing with creators in exile. Fashion designers like Kenzo, Hanae Mori, Yoji Yamamoto, Issy Miyake and Rei Kawakubo are opening up towards Europe and this is reflected in what the Japanese are wearing these days.

Modern Japan is pervaded with a sense of the cosmopolitan. The old East-West antagonism is dying out. Contemporary design, in the shape of Isozaki's architecture or Yamamoto's fashions, is forging an aesthetic unity overlaid with Japanese tradition and the lessons of the West. Cultural assimilation has penetrated deep into the Japanese character; after all, one of the abiding traits of the Japanese spirit has been their capacity to play on this ambiguity. Japan goes through cycles of opening up to outside influences, then turning in on itself to assimilate those influences. Japan is never a slave to its outside models. It manages to absorb foreign inputs quickly enough to preserve its own personality. Japan is a country without ruins and does not have the same reverence for old things which we have. Europe's sense of its automotive mythology goes back to the turn of the century, whereas Japan has no such concerns; it is outside time.

Subaru F624 Estremo, Frankfurt, 1987. Four-door saloon with front-mounted flat six 24-valve turbo engine. Four-wheel drive, four-wheel steering.

Subaru Jo-Car, Tokyo 1987. Compact sports car with centrally-mounted 550 cc engine, automatic electronic variable ratio transmission, four-wheel drive.

Subaru BLT, Tokyo 1987. One-piece car for "business/leisure/transport", 1.2 litre engine, four-wheel drive, four-wheel steering.

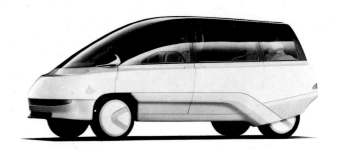

Daihatsu TA-X80, Frankfurt 1987. Small saloon with centrally-mounted V6 996 cc engine, 130 hp, four-wheel drive, hydropneumatic suspension, length 390 cm, Cx 0.25.

Daihatsu Trek, Tokyo 1985. Leisure vehicle which doubles as accommodation, with canvas tent fitting over the upper structure. Length 320 cm.

Daihatsu Urbanbuggy, Tokyo 1987. All-road and town unitary construction vehicle, three-cylinder engine 993 cc, 105 hp, four-wheel drive, length 352 cm, wheels 215 SR 15.

# H O N D A

**Of all the Japanese manufacturers, Honda shows the greatest mastery of styling, a fact recognised even by those who hold Japanese design in contempt.**

oichiro Honda was the son of a blacksmith, a cheerful "dunce" who was crazy about all things mechanical. Once he had made enough of a name for himself with motorbikes, he started on cars in 1962. Honda raised the image of the whole of Japanese industry with their technology, and now they are using design to further the process. Honda is active on all fronts; with three teams of designers round the world – in Japan, in California and in Europe – they can cover every shade of taste in the market, from the most restrained to the most revolutionary. The first milestone in the history of Honda style was the City (exported as the Jazz) launched in 1981 with a high-line passenger compartment based on the *tall boy* concept. Five years later the designers did a U-turn with a super-low-line second-generation City! Honda adapts to all the subtleties of its customers in every continent and in every setting. At the top end, it plays the conservative card with its Legend, while in the small car range, it takes a chance on innovation with the one-piece Today. As for mid-range models, Honda takes a broad sweep; the Civic range which came out in 1983 includes no less than four distinct body styles: a conventional saloon, a more modern hatchback saloon, the high-line Shuttle estate and the CRX sports coupé. At Honda, engineers and designers are playing from the same score, with perfect intonation and no fluffed notes.

Honda City, Tokyo 1981; Turbo II version. Compact car with raised passenger compartment, mass-produced. Engine 1.2 litres turbo, 110 hp. Length 342 cm, height 146 cm.
Honda Civic, Sketch for the three-door version launched in September 1983.

Honda Today, Tokyo 1985. Unitary construction town car, two-cylinder 546 cc engine, 31 hp, length 320 cm, height 131 cm.

Preceding double page:
Nissan Arc-X, Tokyo 1987.
Four-door saloon.
Transverse V6 engine, 3
litres, 24 valves, 190 hp.
Four-wheel drive, four-
wheel steering, length 477
cm. Cx 0.26.

Nissan NX-21, Tokyo 1983.
Five-seater saloon with
gull-wing doors designed
by Nissan Design
International in San Diego.
Rear-mounted ceramic
turbine engine, 100 hp.
Length 452 cm, Cx 0.25.

Nissan Cue-X, Tokyo 1985.
Classic four-door saloon,
front-mounted V6 turbo
engine, 24 valves, 3 litres,

300 hp. Integrated
transmission. Length 486
cm, Cx 0.24.

Nissan Be-1, Tokyo 1985.
Limited production city car
produced in 1987. Based on
the mechanical structure of

the March. Four cylinders,
987 cc, 52 hp, length 363
cm. Plastic body.

**These days Nissan designers are capable of coming up with solutions to every trend and can even persuade the marketing men to accept them.**

The turning point came at the 1988 Tokyo Motor Show. Nissan made a big splash when it unveiled seven prototypes and proved that the creative power of its designers could work in every direction. The seven vehicles covered all possible future developments in the car industry: the post-modern Pao, the Jura family car, the egocentric Saurus, the Judo fun car, the S-Cargo utility vehicle, the sporty Mid-4 and, to crown the collection, the superb Arc-X saloon.

Nissan styling used to be rather clumsy but it has since become brilliant ever since a very daring management allowed the company to bring ground-breaking new designs to the market. The styling of the Prairie (1982), the Pulsar EXA (1986) and the Be-1 (1987) might well be open to discussion, but these were extraordinary demonstrations of commercial daring. These were not cars responding to some predigested marketing ploy for the simple reason that they had no marketing precedent. The Prairie was a roomy, progressive high-line estate car with sliding doors which evoked the design of the Toyota MP-1 unveiled in 1975. The Pulsar EXA revived the Prima modular car design presented by Ford in 1976 with the same concept of an interchangeable rear section to enable the car to be

Above: <u>Mid-4</u>, Tokyo 1987.
Small saloon with centrally-
mounted 3 litre V6 turbo
engine, 330 hp, four-wheel
drive, length 430 cm, Cx
0.30.

Below: <u>Pao</u>, Tokyo 1987.
Country vehicle, length 371
cm.

Above: <u>Jura</u>, Tokyo, 1987.
Unitary construction
vehicle with 2 litre engine
and four-wheel drive,
length 442 cm.

Below and preceding
double page: <u>Arc X</u>, Tokyo
1987. Four-door saloon
designed by Shigeru Miki.
Car Design Award 1987.

transformed into a coupé, estate or pick-up.

Nissan's policy of giving design such a priority is unique in the world car industry, as proven once again by the Be-1, with its 1960s *New Wave* feel. Unveiled on an experimental basis in 1985, it received such a warm welcome that the management agreed to put it on the market. A year later in January 1987, Nissan started to deliver the first of a limited run of 10,000 vehicles and opened a "Be-1" boutique in Tokyo to merchandise clothes and other products.

Nissan's analysis of American taste is no less judicious. It is in the hands of the Nissan Design International Studio, which has been operating in San Diego since it was set up in 1979 and has already produced the NX-21 turbine prototype, the EXA mentioned above and the all-terrain Terrano. In just a few short years Nissan has made up all lost ground, as demonstrated amply by the Silvia and the Prairie launched in 1988.

Such spectacular progress is a measure of just how fast the Japanese revolution has taken place, and with one unique feature: both design and marketing are equally keen on innovation.

**When you have started with nothing and done everything, when good fortune is no longer just luck, when dreams are the only way of getting away from the pragmatism of the car industry, that is the time when Franco Sbarro emerges from his lair.**

**Super Twelve,** Geneva 1982. Compact car power by two coupled Kawasaki 1300 cc six cylinder engines, 240 hp, length 315 cm.

**Shahin 1000 Biturbo,** Geneva 1984. Coupé with gull-wing doors built on the basis of a Mercedes-Benz 500 SEC. 6.9 litre V8 engine, 286 hp.

Franco Sbarro cannot be classified. Is he a coachbuilder, a mechanic or a craftsman? No, Franco Sbarro is simply a dream-maker. Just imagine the following scene: a few yellowing, feathery palm trees trembling in the heat haze, in California, on the French Riviera or in Riyadh. A doubting man wonders how he can turn a handful of dollars into a car and remembers the good old days when coachbuilders could turn their customers' fantasies into reality. The days of Figoni, Saoutchik, Erdmann & Rossi. But on the threshold of the 21st century, who is still equal to the task of satisfying these whims of a bygone era? He is the only one with what it takes to perk up a jaded millionaire, to concoct an all-roads monster, an explosive town car or the exact replica of a great classic.

Picture a huge hangar filled with the pungent smell of polyester, with a jumble of mechanical parts from all over the place mingled with gleaming body panels in methodical disorder. In the depths of a little office, Franco Sbarro is sketching a few clumsy lines amidst a stiffling collection of magazines, plans, files and relief drawings of suspensions. These few lines are the beginnings of an idea to meet the hopes of a potential customer. Franco Sbarro is never out of his saffron-coloured mechanic's overalls, fifteen hours a day. One minute he is taking a telephone call from Abu Dhabi, the next he is giving a quick twist of a screwdriver on a turbo and everywhere at once, running ceaselessly between the three floors of his workshop, finding a solution to every problem. A week passes and the customer returns to sign a fat cheque. This advance gives Sbarro the wherewithal to start designing the prototype. This is the way he works. Each of Sbarro's creations is the fruit of a meeting of two enthusiasts, the result of mutual trust.

Super Eight, Geneva 1984.
Transverse-mounted V8
3-litre Ferrari 308 GTB
engine, 240 hp.

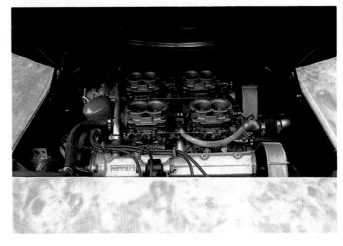

Flashback to 1957, as 18-year-old Franco arrives in Switzerland from far-away Lecce at the foot of the Italian peninsula. He is already stubborn and tireless and quickly finds work as a machinist, then as a breakdown man. The turning point comes in Yverdon when he meets Georges Filipinetti, a great collector and owner of a racing stable who also happens to be a Federal minister. Franco restores a few of his cars and becomes chief mechanic of the Scuderia from 1963 to 1967. From this position, he peers deep into the innermost recesses of Ferrari P3s, Ford GT40s and other supercars.

Having been chief mechanic with Ford-France, Sbarro founds his Atelier de Construction Automobile in 1968. From the wings, Françoise Sbarro makes sure that the business does well; she is the one who manages it, looks after public relations, organises supplies and takes care of the paperwork. Family life and professional life are closely linked for the Sbarros. The workshop is just a stone's throw from home and even when he works late into the night, Franco always finds time to keep an eye on Fabrice and Fabian doing their homework.

Things which could become crazy tinkerings in the hands of many less hardened craftsmen are turned into fantastic but coherent objects by Sbarro's hands. He certainly has an insatiable passion for research and he never takes the easy way out, but beyond all that is a solid foundation built on good sense and realism. His fantastic ideas rely on serious experience of cars learned at the race track.

Franco Sbarro has always been a solid advocate of reinforced polyester resin, which is too often denigrated as being supposedly less noble than aluminium. In fact, this synthetic material has strength characteristics which are completely competitive

Challenge, Geneva 1985. Berlinetta with centrally-mounted 5-litre Mercedes-Benz V8 turbo engine, 380 hp. Four-wheel drive, length 422 cm, speed 290 kph.

Challenge

# SBARRO

and from a practical point of view, *fibreglass* is more suitable for the type of one-off productions which are Sbarro's speciality. Workers are constantly refining the bodywork, smoothing down sharp angles and filling in places where the line is too deep.

Franco Sbarro does not regard himself as a designer and besides, the stylist Camille Diebold often comes in to assist him. He has built several "replicas" drawn from old models, provid

ing ammunition for those detractors who do not regard him as a creator. In much the same way, transforming production cars could be classified as mere "customisation". An example of the latter is the "El Adja" coupé, produced from a Mercedes-Benz 500 SEC in 1984.

However, there is no denying that a true "Sbarro" style has emerged over the years. It is a style which has developed in very different areas which show that Sbarro has always managed to detect the winds of change. His response to the fashion for four-wheel drive vehicles in 1987 was the Monster G, an enormous 4x4 mounted on Boeing wheels. Sbarro indulged his taste for touring saloons in 1985 with the Challenge, powered by a Mercedes engine with integrated transmission. This pointed, mono-lithic design is characterised by a bonnet which seems to be extended by the windscreen and cut short by the rounded rear end.

The lines which Franco likes are always sensual and it is perhaps his compact saloons which best express this. The Super Twelve and the Super Eight have the same extremely compact dimensions (just over three metres), the same ample form and the same breathtaking acceleration; this is provided by two coupled Kawasaki 1300 6 cylinder engines in the former, and by a Ferrari V8 from a 308 GTB in the latter. The Robur, built in 1987, is a variation on the same theme with an even more oval line and a centrally-mounted transverse Audi 200 Turbo engine. By way of an anecdote, Sbarro has dreamed up a gadget to facilitate parking in tight spaces: retractable mini-undercarriage fitted to the back of the car.

This might seem to be little more than a tongue-in-cheek fantasy, but it may be regarded as a symbolic provocation. Cars are an endless field of investigation for everybody who sees them as a fabulous vehicle of freedom and independence. Franco Sbarro is nothing more than one element in this multifaceted picture. There are several hundred lonely craftsmen, utopian visionaries, superstar designers and faceless stylists working from the anonymity of research department; all of them are busy dreaming up forms and concepts to bring new life to cars.

These men hold a few of the keys to the passions which we shall feel in years to come. This book is intended as a homage to them.

Monster G, Geneva, 1987. All-road vehicle with 6.9 litre V8 Mercedes-Benz engine, four-wheel drive, length 460 cm. Wheels from a Boeing 747.

Robur, Geneva, 1988.
Compact saloon powered
by centrally-mounted five-
cylinder Audi 200 Turbo, 200
hp, automatic transmission,
length 330 cm. Rear-
mounted retractable
undercarriage mounted
transversely to facilitate
parking.

**Tomorrow's cars rely more than ever on the teaching of design, so we shall round off this review of contemporary styling with a close-up of a school which sets a fine example.**

The Château de Sully in Tour-de-Peilz near Vevey in Switzerland, home of Art Center Europe.

A design to replace the BX financed by Citroën, produced by the students of the ACCD in Pasadena and presented at the Art Center Europe in March 1987.

For us to single out one school rather than another is very unfair. However, having mentioned many institutions scattered around the world, we are putting the spotlight on the Art Center Europe because both its strengths and its weaknesses are significant in more than one way. The Art Center Europe is an offshoot of the Art Center College of Design, which was founded in Los Angeles in 1930 and has been located in the hills of Pasadena since 1976. The Americans pondered on France and Italy before settling on a country which was more peaceful, both in political and in financial terms. So the Art Center decided to settle near Vevey on the shores of Lake Geneva; the whole operation was supported by the nearby Nestlé company and the Union des Banques Suisses. In California, the school occupies a very contemporary piece of metal architecture, whereas in Switzerland it is installed in the Château de Sully, a baroque folly dating from the last century. The Art Center Europe has been operating since the beginning of the academic year in September 1986; Jo Henry is the director, and the president is David Brown, successor to Don Kubly. Teaching is the responsibility of Uwe Bahnsen, former vice-president of design at Ford-Europe. The course comprises a six-month foundation programme followed by eight semesters leading to a diploma. Four specialities are offered at Vevey: advertising, graphics, product design and transport.

The Art Center does not enjoy universal admiration, but its supporters quote convincing success figures: 50% of Detroit designers have a diploma from Pasadena and factories the world over stock up there. The Japanese throng to Pasadena whereas the Germans are becoming familiar with the road to Vevey. The list of consultants includes Mario Bellini, Giorgetto Giugiaro, Ferdinand Alexander Porsche, Gianni Bulgari and Sergio Pininfarina, not forgetting Xavier Karcher, managing director of Citroën.

The fact that these personalities are present is not just their way of backing the Art Center. These are men with one foot in the future; they know that the patterns of 21st century life are already being drawn in design schools, both in the Art Center and others.

# INDEX

# INDEX